Sticky Fingers
and
Tenderloins

Grilling Ribs, Steaks and Other Tasty Treats

Ted Reader

VIKING
CANADA

VIKING CANADA

Published by the Penguin Group

Penguin Group (Canada), 90 Eglinton Avenue East, Suite 700, Toronto, Ontario, Canada M4P 2Y3
    (a division of Pearson Canada Inc.)

Penguin Group (USA) Inc., 375 Hudson Street, New York, New York 10014, U.S.A.
Penguin Books Ltd, 80 Strand, London WC2R 0RL, England
Penguin Ireland, 25 St Stephen's Green, Dublin 2, Ireland (a division of Penguin Books Ltd)
Penguin Group (Australia), 250 Camberwell Road, Camberwell, Victoria 3124, Australia
    (a division of Pearson Australia Group Pty Ltd)
Penguin Books India Pvt Ltd, 11 Community Centre, Panchsheel Park, New Delhi – 110 017, India
Penguin Group (NZ), cnr Airborne and Rosedale Roads, Albany, Auckland 1310, New Zealand
    (a division of Pearson New Zealand Ltd)
Penguin Books (South Africa) (Pty) Ltd, 24 Sturdee Avenue, Rosebank, Johannesburg 2196, South Africa

Penguin Books Ltd, Registered Offices: 80 Strand, London WC2R 0RL, England

First published 2001

(WEB)   15 14 13 12 11 10 9 8

Copyright © Ted Reader, 2001

Printed and bound in Canada.

NATIONAL LIBRARY OF CANADA CATALOGUING IN PUBLICATION

Reader, Ted
    Sticky fingers and tenderloins : grilling ribs, steaks, and other tasty treats / Ted Reader.

Includes index.
ISBN 0-670-04362-1

1. Barbecue cookery. 2. Cookery. I. Title.

TX840.B3R425   2002   641.7'6   C2002-903703-4

Visit the Penguin Group (Canada) website at **www.penguin.ca**

Special and corporate bulk purchase rates available; please see
www.penguin.ca/corporatesales or call 1-800-810-3104, ext. 477 or 474

I dedicate this book to the love of my life, the wonderful Pamela, whose love and support are what give me the inspiration to cook. You are always in my thoughts. Your smile, your beautiful eyes and of course your strength are my loves.

Let's get sticky.

With all my love,
Your peanut butter bear

Acknowledgments

I cook with my heart and soul. My passion arrives not just from within but from all those whom I have had the pleasure to encounter. If I were to acknowledge all, my list would be as long as one of my grocery shopping lists. Because space is limited, I want to thank the following:

My family, whose love and encouragement know no boundaries, and especially my mother, Astrida, and father, Alex, whose support has been without question. Thank you.

My niece Jessica, who has worked with me on the set of *Cottage Country* as well as on the race circuit with Patrick Racing. You scrubbed a lot of pots and pans and chopped a lot of vegetables, always with a smile. You are a pleasure to work with, and your help is appreciated.

Nicole de Montbrun of Prentice Hall Canada: thank you for believing in me and providing me with the opportunity to be creative and a little crazy.

Per Kristensen, the master artist of the edible photograph.

Chef Olaf Mertens — you can cook, baby!

Chef Luther Miller, a crazy Canuck chef with a passion for flavour and a little beer.

Chef Melanie Dunkelman, you are my kook-a-munga friend. I appreciate all your help on *Cottage Country*. You make my recipes special.

Chef Dale McCarthy, chef daddio, you are the stern chef, a man of detail and precision. Thank you for all of your help in providing food for the many.

Ron McAvan, my friend and associate. If only I could make as many delicious retail sauces as you. You are a master of sauce.

Steven Mintz, the owner of Uni Foods, whose knowledge and love of ribs have given me the inspiration to keep on creating great rib recipes and products.

Bob Butz, freelance food writer and author of *GQ's* "Steak Recipe" article.

Tones Brothers Spices, the greatest dried herbs and spices in the world. Thanks, Thane and company.

Ponderosa Forge in Swift Current—Thank you for the beautifully made shrimp skewers (see photo insert) and steak turner. Great stuff!

Shaun Oakey, the editor who made my recipes sing.

And lastly, to all my friends and family … Cheers, and thanks a lot!

Contents

Introduction

My passion for grilling began when I was young. Memories of my father grilling a 3-inch-thick 4-lb. sirloin steak over white-hot coals make my mouth water still. That old charcoal grill was ancient by the time I was born. It was layered with rust but seasoned with intense flavours.

Eventually that old grill melted, or rusted through, and an air of excitement filled our home at the prospect of getting a new grill. Not! Dad presented us with his new model: a big red wheelbarrow from the garden, filled with charcoal and topped with an old refrigerator shelf for a grill. Embarrassment set in. We were the shame of the neighbourhood. How could I have friends over for a barbecue? The humiliation went on and on. My entire high school years were filled with wheelbarrow-grilled foods. Embarrassing — but truly delicious. Finally, after years of listening to our begging, my father bought a brand-new gas grill. We had made it to the big leagues!

Embarrassed as I was in those years, we always had a delicious meal. I have come to realize that it is not the equipment but what you do with it. Tender juicy steaks, succulent golden chicken breasts, smoky Atlantic salmon — they're just as good whether grilled on the fanciest new gas model or in an old wheelbarrow.

Sticky Fingers and Tenderloins is a collection of my favourite grilling recipes derived from my twenty-five years of cooking — from early days in Whistler, B.C., where barbecued salmon on the side of the ski hill was a lunchtime favourite, to grilling tender steaks at the Olde School in Brantford, Ontario, to my busy days at the SkyDome Hotel in Toronto where baseball-themed menus were a challenging feast for thousands. More recently, as a chef for President's Choice® I was able to enhance my grilling knowledge by developing new grilled foods. I travelled to assorted grill competitions to taste all of the wonderful flavour sensations, and worked on the recipes for the *Dave Nichol Cookbook* and the *President's Choice® Barbecue Cookbook*.

But my love for the grill truly unfolded when I became the barbecue guy on *Cottage Country Television*, creating recipes for planked salmon, hay-wrapped steak, grilled Caesar salad, shrimp parfait and the ridiculous foot-high burger. *Cottage Country* allowed me to be crazy *and* grill.

This book will take you into a world of new flavours as you try recipes that may seem a little bizarre but are a lot of fun to cook — and even more fun to eat. I believe that when you grill there really are no rules. Experimenting with a variety of flavours will only make you a better griller.

I have tried to put together a collection of recipes that everyone can use, from simple recipes to advanced. I try to use ingredients that you can easily find in your favourite grocery store, but sometimes you may have to search for something in specialty food shops or markets.

Sometimes the best part of a meal is the beginning, and "Heavenly Beginnings" includes recipes for soups, salads and appetizers. A hot bowl of soup, whether it is a charred corn chowder or a creamy pumpkin soup, warms the soul and fills the belly. Hearty soups are often meals in themselves. I love to dunk a piece of grilled bread into a hot bowl of soup.

I have made many salads on the set of *Cottage Country*, because salads are a great accompaniment to any grilled meal. They are often light and refreshing and highlight the best flavours of the summer. Salads also make the perfect side dish for any grilled entrée. Tangy coleslaw is the perfect side for ribs, and potato salad makes a steak complete. Planked salmon sizzles for a cucumber salad, and a fruit salad is a perfect topping for ice cream. A meal at my house just isn't complete without a great salad, especially when it's dressed with my favourite Russian dressing.

First impressions are always important, and appetizers are the introduction to a perfect meal. Grilled Chicken Yakitori or Cinnamon-Skewered Lamb Kebabs are a sweet beginning to any meal. My favourite appetizers are the Margarita Wings sizzling with lime and tequila, and my Jumbo Shrimp Parfait, a truly spectacular presentation with big flavours and a ton of shrimp. For those who are a little crazy, try the Infiniti Dip, with 25-plus layers of cheese, salsas and guacamole, a crazy dip that may become addictive.

"Sultry Sides" are the dishes that enhance and complete your main courses. A grilled steak is not complete without a baked potato loaded with butter, sour cream, chives, bacon bits and cheese. Baby back ribs need some creamy macaroni and cheese, and grilled chicken just isn't complete without some tender grilled vegetables. My personal favourite is sautéed mushrooms and onions tossed with crumbled blue cheese. No recipe necessary for this side dish; you just need lots of mushrooms, sweet onions and a ton of crumbled blue cheese. Sides are often forgotten about, but to me they are the most important part of a grilled meal.

"Finger Lickin'" is one of my favourite chapters. I love a great sandwich. I actually believe that sandwiches are their own food group. A really good sandwich

begins with fresh bread. If you bake your own bread, that is the best, but if not look for a good bakery to provide you with the best-flavoured rolls and loaves. Roasted garlic and rosemary baguette or a black olive sourdough works great in a grilled steak sandwich. A soft onion roll is a perfect base to grilled chicken or grilled vegetables, and an egg roll is the best base for your favourite sausage or hot dog. The second most important part of a sandwich is the main ingredient: grilled steak, smoked chicken or turkey, planked salmon, pulled pork, bratwurst or a hamburger. And the final part of a sandwich is the garnish and condiments. Roasted chipotle mayonnaise, hot and spicy mustard, grilled vegetables, ketchup, relish, sauerkraut, pickles and fresh lettuce and tomatoes are only a few of the ingredients that make the sandwich a sandwich. Flavour is what it is all about. The more flavour, the tastier a sandwich will be.

"Rubbin' Is Lovin'" is a collection of seasoning blends. Rubs and pastes of assorted herbs and spices bring out and enhance the flavours of grilled foods. I use these rub recipes throughout the book, but if you don't have time to make your own, go ahead and substitute your favourite store-bought products.

"Rib Stickin'" is the bone-sucking section of finger-licking rib recipes to make your mouth water and your fingers sticky. Pork ribs, beef ribs and lamb ribs are the kings of the barbecue. When slowly cooked, then grilled and slathered with your favourite BBQ sauce, the meat will be truly tender and fall off the bone. There are many ways to cook ribs. My favourite is braising, but you can also boil, steam, slowly grill, roast or smoke them. However you choose to prepare your ribs, remember that they need to be tender. Nothing spoils a barbecue like tough ribs.

"Tender Loins" is the real meat of this book. Great-flavoured steaks of beef, veal, pork, lamb and game are the essence of grilling. This chapter includes a guide to cuts of steaks. Steak is probably one of the easiest foods to grill, and my Hand Touch Method to test for doneness makes it even easier. I love a great steak; my favourite is a thick-cut rib-eye seasoned with a few tablespoons of my Great Canadian Steak Spice and grilled rare. I recall once waking up in the middle of the night after dreaming of the steak that I had eaten that night at the Chicago Chop House. It was a 24-oz. bone-in rib-eye seasoned with Cajun spices and grilled to medium-rare. It melted in my mouth like butter. I woke up in the middle of the night salivating!

Chicken is one of the most popular meats to grill, and "Breasts and Thighs" is a collection of some interesting and flavourful recipes. The kicker in this chapter is Devil's Brewed Roast Chicken, in which the whole chicken is seasoned and then an open can of beer is inserted in the rump, allowing the bird to stand up. Slowly grill roasted, the bird steams from the beer on the inside and gets crispy on the outside. It not only looks dramatic but also is delicious. Chicken breasts can be marinated in virtually anything and then grilled to perfection. Chicken thighs are the tastiest, especially when glazed with a spicy sauce. Wings and drumsticks make a perfect picnic food as well as great appetizers.

I am often asked why chicken burns so easily on the grill. One reason is that the skin of the chicken is fatty, but more often it is because the grill temperature is too high. Keep your grill between medium and medium-high and keep the lid open (unless slow roasting or smoking).

You may have to move the chicken pieces to a cooler spot on the grill, but be patient: chicken must be well done. Lastly, glaze the chicken pieces with sauce during the final minutes of cooking rather than at the beginning.

If you like grilled seafood, the recipes in "Wet 'n' Wild" are mouth-watering. Seafood is not always the easiest to grill, but with my recipes I hope to make you a fan of it. My signature recipe for seafood is planked salmon, a truly simple procedure that gives excellent results every time. Planking works well for other seafood — try haddock, sea bass or scallops on a plank. The options are endless and the flavours incredible. Try jumbo shrimp stuffed with crab meat, sugarcane-skewered grilled swordfish or cinnamon-skewered sea scallops with peach salsa. My award-winning grilled oysters with bacon mango BBQ sauce is one of my all-time grilling favourites, so easy to prepare and absolutely delicious.

"Decadent Delights" is for the sweet at heart. Grilled desserts are a real treat at any barbecue and can easily be prepared in advance. Slow roasted pineapple is a wonderful recipe that goes great with ice cream, and leftovers can be cut up into cubes and used in a BBQ sauce. Lydia's Banana Boats is a rich grilled banana dessert perfect for kids. But my favourite is a strawberry and rhubarb crisp grill baked in a cast-iron pan. Served hot or cold with ice cream, it is a summertime hit.

I hope that you enjoy *Sticky Fingers and Tenderloins*. It was my pleasure to create, test and taste each of these recipes, and I hope they bring you as much excitement and enjoyment as they do me.

Ted Reader

Sticky Fingers and Tenderloins

Heavenly Beginnings

Soups

Salads

Appetizers

Corn Chowder with Truly the Very Best Atlantic Lobster Cakes

Here is my tribute to the lobster trappers of the East Coast. Canadian lobster is truly delicious—and a reasonable price.

3 tbsp.	butter	4 cups	fresh peaches and cream
1	large onion, diced		corn kernels (from about
3 cloves	garlic, finely chopped		6 ears of corn)
2 cups	Yukon Gold potatoes cut in	2 tbsp.	chopped fresh thyme
	½-inch cubes	¾ cup	whipping cream
1 tbsp.	Bone Dust BBQ Spice (page 97)		Salt and pepper
4 to 6 cups	chicken, vegetable or lobster stock		Sprigs of fresh dill, for garnish

Tip

To give the chowder a great charred flavour, grill the cobs of corn for 5 to 8 minutes, turning, until slightly charred and golden brown. Then use a sharp knife to scrape the grilled kernels from the cob.

1. In a large soup pot melt the butter over medium heat. Add the onion and garlic; cook for 3 to 4 minutes or until tender.

2. Add the potatoes; cook for another 3 to 4 minutes.

3. Add the BBQ spice and stock. Bring to a boil, reduce heat and simmer the soup, uncovered and stirring occasionally, for 45 minutes or until the potatoes are soft and the soup is thickened. If necessary, add a little more stock to thin the soup.

4. While the soup is simmering, make the lobster cakes.

5. Add the corn and thyme to the soup; continue to simmer for 15 minutes.

6. Whip the cream until it's just thickened and fold into the hot soup. Adjust seasoning with salt and pepper.

7. To serve, place 1 lobster cake in the centre of each of 8 large soup plates. Pour ¾ cup of corn chowder around the cake. Garnish with sprigs of fresh dill.

SERVES 8

Truly the Very Best Atlantic Lobster Cakes

In this recipe you can also use fresh crab meat or even shredded whitefish like cod or haddock. These cakes are also wonderful on their own served with a little remoulade sauce or spicy mayonnaise.

½ cup	mayonnaise	1 tsp.	chopped garlic
1	egg	½ tsp.	ground cumin
2	green onions, thinly sliced	½ tsp.	curry powder
1 tbsp.	chopped fresh cilantro	1½ lb.	cooked Atlantic lobster meat
1 tbsp.	chopped fresh dill		Salt, pepper and Louisiana hot sauce
1 tbsp.	lemon juice	1½ cups	coarsely ground whole wheat
1 tsp.	Bay Seasoning (page 98)		cracker crumbs

1. Preheat oven to 375°F.

2. In a large bowl whisk together the mayonnaise, egg, green onions, cilantro, dill, lemon juice, Bay Seasoning, garlic, cumin and curry.

3. Gently fold in the cooked lobster meat. Season to taste with salt, pepper and Louisiana hot sauce.

4. Add the cracker crumbs and gently mix until everything binds together loosely.

5. Form into 8 small cakes. You can use an ice cream scoop to make this a little easier.

6. Place lobster cakes on a lightly greased baking sheet and bake for 10 to 12 minutes or until heated through.

SERVES 8

Helluva Halloween Pumpkin Soup

I love Halloween, and nothing is more in season than the pumpkin. Linus believed in the Great Pumpkin, and I believe that if Linus had had this soup he would have seen the Great Pumpkin for sure.

3 lb.	fresh pumpkin flesh cut into 2-inch chunks	2	jalapeño peppers, seeded and finely chopped
¼ cup	olive oil	8 cups	chicken stock
1 tsp.	cinnamon	1 tbsp.	chopped fresh sage
1 tsp.	cayenne pepper	1 cup	whipping cream
2 tsp.	salt		Salt and freshly ground
3 tbsp.	butter		black pepper
4 cloves	garlic, chopped	½ cup	orange blossom honey
1	large yellow onion, chopped	½ cup	sour cream
		8	5-inch cinnamon sticks

1. Preheat oven to 375°F.

2. In a roasting pan toss together the pumpkin chunks, oil, cinnamon, cayenne and salt. Roast for 45 to 60 minutes or until the pumpkin is lightly roasted and tender. Set aside.

3. In a large soup pot melt the butter over medium-high heat. Sauté the garlic, onion and jalapeño peppers for 3 to 5 minutes, stirring occasionally, until translucent and tender.

4. Add the roasted pumpkin and chicken stock. Bring to a rolling boil, reduce heat to medium-low and simmer, uncovered and stirring occasionally, for 20 to 30 minutes or until tender. Using a hand blender or food processor, purée the soup until smooth.

5. Add the sage and cream. Return soup to a boil, and season to taste with salt and pepper.

6. Serve immediately garnished with a drizzling of orange blossom honey, a dollop of sour cream and a cinnamon swizzle stick.

SERVES 8

French-Canadian Roasted Onion Soup with Maple Syrup and Oka Cheese

One of the most popular soups is French onion soup, a rich soup created with slowly caramelized onions, red wine and beef broth and garnished with a crisp crouton topped with melted Gruyère cheese. This is my version of the classic using unpasteurized Oka cheese from my friends at Agropur Cheeses.

6	large sweet onions, sliced	¼ cup	Quebec maple syrup
12 cloves	garlic, finely chopped	2 tbsp.	chopped fresh herbs (any combination of
1 tsp.	ground cumin		parsley, sage, rosemary, thyme or savory)
1 tsp.	chili powder	2	bay leaves
¼ cup +		1 tsp.	cracked black peppercorns
2 tbsp.	olive oil	8 cups	beef broth
	Salt and pepper	16 slices	French bread
½ cup	Canadian whisky	2 cups	shredded Oka cheese

1. Preheat oven to 375°F.

2. In a roasting pan mix together the onions, garlic, cumin, chili powder and ¼ cup of the olive oil. Season to taste with salt and pepper. Roast onion mixture, stirring occasionally, for 45 to 60 minutes or until slightly charred and tender.

3. In a large soup pot heat the remaining 2 tbsp. olive oil over medium-high heat. Add the roasted onion mixture and sauté for 10 minutes, stirring constantly.

4. Deglaze the onions with the whisky. Stand back as you add the whisky, as it may flambé. Stir to scrape up any brown bits. Add the maple syrup, fresh herbs, bay leaves, peppercorns, beef broth and salt to taste. Bring to a rolling boil, reduce heat to medium-low and simmer, stirring occasionally, for 30 minutes. Adjust seasoning with salt and pepper. Discard bay leaves.

5. Preheat broiler. On a baking sheet, lightly toast the bread slices on both sides to make croutons.

6. Ladle soup into 8 ovenproof crocks. Top each with 2 croutons and ¼ cup of Oka cheese. Broil for 3 to 5 minutes or until the cheese melts and bubbles. Serve immediately.

SERVES 8

Half-Baked Potato Soup

For this hearty winter soup I use large Yukon Gold potatoes and bake them until they are half baked — tender on the outside but still hard in the centre.

6	large Yukon Gold potatoes	**GARNISHES**	
2 tbsp.	coarse kosher salt	1 cup	sour cream
¼ cup	butter	1 cup	crumbled crisp bacon
1	large yellow onion, finely diced	½ cup	shredded yellow Cheddar cheese
4 cloves	garlic, minced	½ cup	shredded Gruyère cheese
2 stalks	celery, finely diced	4	green onions, thinly sliced
1	leek, including pale green part, thinly sliced	½	small red onion, diced
8 cups	chicken stock	1	pkg. (200 g) Hickory Sticks Smoked Flavour potato matchsticks
1 cup	whipping cream		
1 tbsp.	chopped fresh thyme		
	Salt and freshly ground black pepper		

1. Preheat oven to 425°F.

2. Wash and scrub potatoes. Season wet potatoes with coarse kosher salt; roast for 45 minutes or until still a little firm in the centre. Let cool for 30 minutes. Cut potatoes into 1-inch chunks.

3. In a large soup pot melt the butter over medium-high heat. Sauté the onion, garlic, celery and leek for 4 to 5 minutes, stirring occasionally, or until translucent and tender.

4. Add the potatoes and chicken stock. Bring to a rolling boil, reduce heat to medium-low and simmer, stirring occasionally to prevent sticking, for 30 to 40 minutes or until thick. Purée the soup in a blender or food processor.

5. Return soup to heat. Add cream and thyme; simmer for 10 minutes more. Season to taste with salt and pepper.

6. To serve, ladle soup into 8 large soup bowls. Garnish with a large dollop of sour cream, a generous sprinkle of bacon bits, shredded Cheddar and Gruyère cheese, green onions, red onion and Hickory Sticks.

SERVES 8

Cedar-Planked Salmon Chowder

If one was to say that I had a signature dish, it would be cedar-planked salmon. I have planked salmon as well as hundreds of other foods. I love salmon and believe that the only way to perfectly cook it every time is to plank it.

This recipe is a variation on the classic recipe from my *Sticks and Stones Cookbook: The Art of Grilling on Plank, Vine and Stone.*

Cedar-Planked Salmon

6	Atlantic salmon fillets (each 6 oz.), skinned	Special equipment: 1 untreated cedar plank (at least 12 x 12 inches and ½- to ¾-inch thick), soaked in water overnight
¼ cup	Salmon Seasoning (page 98)	
	Sea salt	
1	lemon, halved	

1. Preheat grill to high.

2. Season salmon fillets with Salmon Seasoning.

3. Sprinkle plank with sea salt. Place plank on the grill and close the lid. Let the plank heat for 3 to 5 minutes or until it starts to crackle.

4. Place the salmon fillets on the plank. Close the lid and bake for 12 to 15 minutes or until the fish flakes easily with a fork. Periodically check the plank; if it is burning, spray it with water.

5. Squeeze the lemon over the salmon.

6. Carefully remove the plank from the grill and transfer salmon to a cutting board. Let salmon cool before adding to chowder.

Continued ...

Salmon Chowder

4 slices	bacon, diced		2 cups	half-and-half cream
3 cloves	garlic, minced		1 tbsp.	chopped fresh dill
1	yellow onion, diced		1 tsp.	lemon zest
2 stalks	celery, diced			Planked salmon (recipe precedes)
3 tbsp.	all-purpose flour			Salt and freshly ground
3 cups	fish stock			black pepper
4	Yukon Gold potatoes, peeled and diced			

1. In a large saucepan over medium-high heat cook the bacon until crisp. Remove with a slotted spoon and set aside. Add the garlic, onion and celery to bacon drippings and sauté for 2 to 3 minutes or until tender. Add the flour and stir until absorbed.

2. Add the fish stock a little at a time, stirring after each addition until smooth.

3. Add the potatoes. Bring to a boil, reduce heat to medium-low and simmer for 20 minutes, stirring occasionally, or until the potatoes are tender.

4. Stir in cream, dill and lemon zest. Return to a slow boil.

5. Cut the cooled planked salmon into ½-inch chunks. Gently stir salmon and reserved bacon bits into chowder. Season to taste with salt and pepper.

6. Serve immediately.

SERVES 8

Grilled Ranch Chicken Soup with Chili Dumplings

Here's a hearty soup that is great for warming the soul.

8	boneless skinless chicken breasts (each 6 oz.)	**CHILI DUMPLINGS**	
2 tbsp.	Bone Dust BBQ Spice (page 97)	2 ½ cups	all-purpose flour
2 tbsp.	vegetable oil	2 tsp.	baking powder
1	lime, juiced	1 tsp.	chili powder
	Salt to taste	1 tsp.	salt
2 tbsp.	butter	1 tbsp.	dried parsley
4 cloves	garlic, minced	¼ tsp.	black pepper
1	onion, diced	¼ cup	vegetable oil
1	leek, diced	½ to	
2 stalks	celery, diced	1 cup	buttermilk
2	carrots, peeled and diced		
2	parsnips, peeled and diced		
2 tbsp.	chopped fresh herbs (parsley, sage and thyme)		
8 cups	chicken stock		

1. In a bowl mix together the chicken breasts, BBQ spice, oil and lime juice. Marinate, covered and refrigerated, for 4 hours.

2. Preheat grill to high.

3. Remove chicken from marinade and season with salt. Grill for 5 to 6 minutes per side or until fully cooked and lightly charred. Cut into 1-inch chunks and set aside.

4. In a large soup pot melt the butter over medium-high heat. Add garlic, onion and leek; sauté for 3 to 4 minutes or until translucent and tender. Add celery, carrots and parsnips; sauté for 4 minutes. Add herbs and chicken stock. Bring to a boil, reduce heat to medium-low and simmer, uncovered and stirring occasionally, for 30 minutes.

Continued ...

5. Meanwhile, prepare the dumplings. Sift the flour, baking powder, chili powder and salt into a large bowl. Stir in the parsley and black pepper. Make a well in the centre and add the oil and ½ cup of the buttermilk. Stir together to make a soft dough, adding more milk if necessary.

6. Add chicken to soup and return to a simmer. Drop 16 spoonfuls of the dumpling batter on top of the simmering soup. Continue to simmer, uncovered, for 8 to 10 minutes or until the dumplings are puffed and cooked through.

7. Serve immediately.

SERVES 8

Chunky Blue Cheese Dressing

My all-time favourite dressing is blue cheese. A steakhouse staple, it goes best with iceberg lettuce, but try it drizzled on grilled steaks or chicken. Use Danish blue or French Roquefort.

1 cup	mayonnaise
1 cup	sour cream
¼ cup	cold water
2 tbsp.	lemon juice
1 cup	crumbled blue cheese
2 tsp.	Worcestershire sauce
½ tsp.	salt
2	green onions, finely chopped
	Freshly ground black pepper

1. In a large bowl whisk together the mayonnaise, sour cream, water and lemon juice.

2. Stir in the blue cheese, Worcestershire sauce, salt and green onions. Season to taste with pepper.

3. Transfer to a sealed container and refrigerate until needed. Will keep up to 1 week.

MAKES ABOUT 3 CUPS

Creamy French Parmesan Dressing

There is a steakhouse in Bentonville, Arkansas, called Fred's. This is my version of their killer Creamy French Parmesan.

1 cup	grated Parmesan cheese
1 cup	mayonnaise
1 cup	sour cream
¼ cup	cold water
¼ cup	white wine vinegar
2 tbsp.	Dijon mustard
2 cloves	garlic, minced
1 tbsp.	chopped fresh thyme
2 tsp.	Worcestershire sauce
1 tsp.	paprika
¼ tsp.	cayenne pepper
	Salt and freshly ground black pepper

1. In a medium bowl whisk together the Parmesan cheese, mayonnaise, sour cream, water, vinegar and mustard.

2. Stir in the garlic, thyme, Worcestershire sauce, paprika and cayenne. Season to taste with salt and pepper.

3. Transfer to a sealed container and refrigerate until needed. Will keep up to 1 week.

MAKES ABOUT 3½ CUPS

Astrida's Lemon Vinaigrette

My mom is a great cook. She makes some wonderful dishes, but I love her lemon vinaigrette the best.

½ cup	lemon juice
2 tbsp.	white vinegar
1 tbsp.	chopped fresh parsley
1 tbsp.	chopped fresh dill
1 tbsp.	sugar
2 tsp.	mustard powder
2 cloves	garlic, minced
1 cup	vegetable oil
	Salt and freshly ground black pepper

1. In a small bowl whisk together the lemon juice, vinegar, parsley, dill, sugar, mustard powder and garlic.

2. While whisking, slowly add the vegetable oil in a steady stream.

3. Season to taste with salt and pepper.

4. Transfer to a sealed container and refrigerate until needed. Will keep up to 1 week.

MAKES ABOUT 1½ CUPS

Russian Dressing

I love the sweet and sour flavours of Russian dressing. Kraft® makes a great Russian dressing, which I like to use in various BBQ sauce recipes. But here's my own for outstanding salads.

½ cup	honey
½ cup	ketchup
¼ cup	white vinegar
1 tbsp.	lemon juice
2 tsp.	paprika
1 tsp.	mustard powder
1 tsp.	celery salt
½ tsp.	cayenne pepper
1 cup	vegetable oil
	Salt and pepper

1. In a medium bowl whisk together the honey, ketchup, vinegar, lemon juice, paprika, mustard powder, celery salt, cayenne and vegetable oil. Season to taste with salt and pepper.

2. Transfer to a sealed container and refrigerate until needed. Will keep up to 1 week.

MAKES ABOUT 2½ CUPS

Green Goddess Ranch Dressing

You do not often see this classic dressing on menus or in the supermarket these days. I think that green goddess was one of the first ranch-type dressings.

1 cup	mayonnaise		¼ cup	chopped fresh parsley
1 cup	sour cream		2 tbsp.	chopped capers
½ cup	buttermilk		1 tbsp.	chopped fresh dill
¼ cup	white vinegar		1 tbsp.	chopped fresh thyme
2 tbsp.	Dijon mustard		1 tsp.	coarsely ground black pepper
1 tbsp.	lemon juice		1 tsp.	Worcestershire sauce
2	anchovy fillets, minced		¼ tsp.	cayenne pepper
1 bunch	green onions, finely chopped			Salt
2 cloves	garlic, minced			

1. In a medium bowl whisk together the mayonnaise, sour cream, buttermilk, vinegar, mustard and lemon juice until smooth.

2. Add the anchovies, green onions, garlic, parsley, capers, dill, thyme, black pepper, Worcestershire sauce and cayenne. Season to taste with salt.

3. Transfer to a sealed container and refrigerate until needed. Will keep up to 1 week.

MAKES ABOUT 3 CUPS

Maple Onion Balsamic Vinaigrette

The key to this dressing is the roasting of the onion prior to making the dressing.

1	large sweet onion, sliced	½ cup	balsamic vinegar
3 cloves	garlic, halved	¼ cup	maple syrup
2 tbsp. +		2 tbsp.	chopped fresh basil
1 cup	olive oil	2 tbsp.	Dijon mustard
	Salt and pepper		

---

1. Preheat oven to 425°F.

2. In a small baking dish toss the onions and garlic with 2 tbsp. of the olive oil. Season to taste with salt and pepper. Roast onions for 30 to 45 minutes or until lightly charred and tender.

3. In a food processor purée the onion mixture. Add the balsamic vinegar, maple syrup, basil and mustard. Turn processor on and add the remaining 1 cup of olive oil in a slow steady stream until the dressing is emulsified.

4. Season to taste with salt and pepper.

5. Transfer to a sealed container and refrigerate until needed. Will keep up to 1 week.

MAKES ABOUT 2 CUPS

Spicy Grilled Jalapeño Dressing

Try this salad dressing on grilled vegetables and as a marinade for chicken or fish.

6	large jalapeño peppers	½ to	
4	shallots, peeled	1 tsp.	sugar
¼ cup	lime juice	½ cup	vegetable oil
1 tbsp.	chopped fresh cilantro		Salt and freshly ground
1 tsp.	Bone Dust BBQ Spice (page 97)		black pepper
1 tsp.	chopped garlic		

---

1. Preheat grill to medium-high.

2. Place the jalapeño peppers and shallots on a grill screen and grill, turning occasionally, until nicely charred. Let cool. Peel and seed the jalapeño peppers.

3. In a food processor purée the jalapeño peppers and shallots until smooth. Add the lime juice, cilantro, BBQ spice, garlic and sugar. Turn on processor and slowly pour in the vegetable oil until dressing is emulsified. Season to taste with salt and pepper.

4. Transfer to a sealed container and refrigerate until needed. Will keep up to 1 week.

MAKES ABOUT 1½ CUPS

Thousand Islands Dressing

Try this dressing as a dip for fresh vegetables as well as drizzled on crisp iceberg lettuce.

1½ cups	mayonnaise		2 tbsp.	chopped gherkins
½ cup	ketchup		2 tbsp.	finely chopped capers
2 tbsp.	lemon juice		1 tbsp.	chopped fresh parsley
1 tbsp.	white vinegar		1 tsp.	mustard powder
3	green onions, chopped		1 tsp.	dried dill
1	small red onion, finely diced		1 tsp.	black pepper
3	anchovies, minced			Salt
2 cloves	garlic, minced			

1. In a bowl whisk together the mayonnaise, ketchup, lemon juice and vinegar. Stir in the green onions, red onion, anchovies, garlic, gherkins, capers, parsley, mustard powder, dill and black pepper. Season to taste with salt.

2. Transfer to a sealed container and refrigerate until needed. Will keep up to 1 week.

MAKES ABOUT 3 CUPS

Roasted Garlic Caesar Dressing

Caesar salad is one of the most popular salads on restaurant menus. Roasting the garlic takes away the sharpness of raw garlic and adds a natural sweetness to the dressing. This dressing is also good as a marinade for grilled chicken.

12	large cloves garlic, peeled	2 tbsp.	red wine vinegar
1½ cups	olive oil	1 tbsp.	Worcestershire sauce
6	anchovies, minced	¼ tsp.	hot sauce
¼ cup	Dijon mustard	½ cup	grated Parmesan cheese
1	lemon, juiced (about ¼ cup)		Salt and pepper

1. Preheat oven to 325°F.

2. Place garlic cloves in an ovenproof dish. Cover with olive oil and roast for 30 to 40 minutes or until the garlic is golden brown and tender. Let cool.

3. Remove the cloves from the oil, reserving the oil, and in a medium bowl mash until smooth.

4. Stir in the anchovies and mustard. While stirring add the lemon juice, vinegar, Worcestershire sauce and hot sauce. Continue stirring and add the reserved roasted garlic oil in a slow steady stream.

5. Stir in the Parmesan cheese and season to taste with salt and pepper.

6. Transfer to a sealed container and refrigerate until needed. Use this dressing on crisp romaine leaves garnished with extra cheese, croutons and crispy bacon bits.

MAKES ABOUT 2½ CUPS

Tip

For a twist, add bacon bits to the dressing and serve as a dip or sauce.

Warm Bacon Mustard Dressing

Not all dressings need to be served cold. This one is meant to be served warm. Prepare it ahead and store in the refrigerator for up to 2 weeks. Warm it in the microwave for 30 to 45 seconds, then enjoy drizzled over fresh spinach or crisp greens.

8 slices	smoked bacon	2 tbsp.	chopped fresh parsley
3 cloves	garlic, minced	1 tbsp.	chopped fresh sage
½ cup	cider vinegar	1½ cups	olive oil
¼ cup	Dijon mustard		Hot sauce
¼ cup	grainy mustard		Salt and pepper
¼ cup	honey		

1. In a large skillet fry the bacon over medium heat until crisp. Drain on paper towels and let cool. Coarsely chop the bacon and set aside.

2. In a bowl whisk together the garlic, vinegar, Dijon mustard, grainy mustard, honey, parsley and sage. While stirring add the olive oil in a steady stream until incorporated. Stir in the reserved bacon. Season to taste with hot sauce, salt and pepper.

3. Transfer to a sealed container and refrigerate until needed. Will keep up to 2 weeks. Reheat before using.

MAKES ABOUT 3 CUPS

Steakhouse Tomato and Sweet Onion Salad with BBQ Dressing

One of my favourite menu items when eating in some of America's greatest steakhouses is a beefsteak tomato and onion salad. I especially like it when the salad is garnished with crumbled French or Danish blue cheese. It is a really easy recipe. All you need is wonderful fresh beefsteak tomatoes and sweet onions — and of course the awesome dressing.

4	large beefsteak tomatoes		**BBQ DRESSING**	
2	large sweet onions (Vidalia, Texas Sweet or Maui)		1	can (28 oz.) plum tomatoes, seeded and drained
	Freshly ground black pepper		2	anchovy fillets
1 tbsp.	chopped fresh basil		1 cup	gourmet BBQ sauce
	Crumbled blue cheese		3 tbsp.	grated horseradish (jarred will do)
			2 tbsp.	cider vinegar
			1 tbsp.	chopped fresh basil
			1 tbsp.	chopped garlic
			2 tsp.	Bone Dust BBQ Spice (page 97)
				Salt and pepper to taste
			½ cup	olive oil

1. Slice the tomatoes into ½-inch-thick rounds. Slice the onions into ¼-inch-thick rounds. On a large platter, alternate slices of tomato and onion. Season with pepper to taste.

2. To make the dressing, place all the ingredients except the oil in a food processor. Pulse until smooth. Turn on the processor and slowly add the olive oil until the dressing is emulsified.

3. Spoon the dressing over the tomato and onion slices. Garnish with chopped basil and crumbled blue cheese.

SERVES 8

Red Beet Salad with Honey Orange Vinaigrette

For a little change to this salad try roasting the beets instead of boiling them. It brings out their natural sweetness.

5	beets, cooked, cooled and peeled	1 tsp.	coarsely ground black pepper
1	onion, thinly sliced	¼ cup	orange juice
1	orange, peeled and cut in segments	3 tbsp.	olive oil
		1 tbsp.	orange blossom honey
1 tbsp.	chopped fresh thyme		Salt

Tip

In season look for golden white beets. Great sweet flavour with a different look!

1. Slice the beets in half lengthwise and then thinly slice crosswise.

2. In a medium bowl, thoroughly combine the beets, onion, orange segments, thyme and pepper.

3. In a small bowl whisk together the orange juice, olive oil and honey. Pour over the beet mixture and mix thoroughly. Season to taste with salt.

4. Chill and serve.

SERVES 8

Grilled New Potato and Cheddar Salad

Buy the smallest red and white new potatoes you can find. This way you may not have to cut the potatoes for the salad. Using a grill basket for the potatoes will make grilling them a lot easier.

1 lb.	mini red new potatoes	1 tbsp.	chopped fresh parsley
1 lb.	mini white new potatoes	1 to 2 tsp.	Bone Dust BBQ Spice (page 97)
1	small red onion, diced	½ cup	mayonnaise
1 cup	shredded yellow Cheddar cheese	2 tbsp.	red wine vinegar
1 tbsp.	chopped garlic	1 tbsp.	Dijon mustard
1 tbsp.	chopped fresh rosemary		Salt and pepper

1. In a large pot of salted water, boil the potatoes for 15 to 20 minutes or until just tender. Drain and cool.

2. Preheat grill to medium-high.

3. If necessary, cut the potatoes into halves or quarters to make bite-sized pieces. Place in a grilling basket and grill for 15 minutes or until lightly charred and tender, turning the basket twice. Transfer potatoes to a large bowl.

4. Add the onion, cheese, garlic, rosemary, parsley and BBQ spice. Mix well.

5. In a small bowl whisk together the mayonnaise, vinegar and mustard. Pour over potato mixture. Season to taste with salt and pepper and mix thoroughly.

6. Chill and serve.

SERVES 8

Grilled Spicy Potato Salad with Tart Apples

The tartness of the apples cools the heat of the poblano chili pepper. Wear rubber gloves when seeding the habanero peppers — they're HOT!

6	Yukon Gold potatoes	**DRESSING**	
1	sweet onion, sliced	1 to 2	
	½-inch thick	(if you dare)	habanero peppers, seeded
1	red bell pepper, sliced	2 tbsp.	lemon juice
	½-inch thick	2 tbsp.	white vinegar
1	poblano pepper, sliced	1 tbsp.	chopped garlic
	½-inch thick	1 tbsp.	chopped fresh cilantro
2 tbsp.	vegetable oil	1 tsp.	sugar
2 tsp.	Bone Dust BBQ Spice (page 97)	⅓ cup	vegetable oil
2	Granny Smith apples		Salt and pepper
1 tbsp.	lemon juice		

1. Cook the potatoes in a pot of boiling salted water for 20 minutes or until just tender. Drain and let cool. Cut potatoes into ½-inch-thick slices.

2. In a bowl gently toss together the potatoes, onion, red pepper, poblano pepper, vegetable oil and BBQ spice. Place vegetables in a grill basket.

3. Cut the apples into 1-inch cubes and toss with the lemon juice to keep the apples from turning brown. Set aside.

4. Preheat grill to high.

5. While the grill is heating, make the dressing. In a food processor purée until smooth the habanero peppers, lemon juice, vinegar, garlic, cilantro and sugar. Slowly add the oil until the dressing is emulsified. Season to taste with salt and pepper.

6. Grill the vegetables, turning occasionally, for 10 to 15 minutes or until slightly charred. Transfer to a large bowl.

7. Drain the apples and add to the vegetables. Pour over the dressing, season to taste and mix thoroughly.

SERVES 8

Green Mango Salad

I first had this truly delicious salad at the Thai Shan Inn Restaurant in Toronto. My version uses President's Choice® Memories of Thailand Fiery Thai Dipping Sauce. This sauce is available only in grocery stores that carry President's Choice® private-label products. You can find a similar sauce in Asian food markets and specialty food stores, but I like the PC one best.

A green mango is an unripe mango. It has a sour flavour — which is why this salad has a sweet dressing.

1	green mango, peeled and pitted	**DRESSING**	
1	red bell pepper, cut into thin strips	¼ cup	President's Choice® Memories of Thailand
1	green bell pepper, cut into		Fiery Thai Dipping Sauce
	thin strips	3 tbsp.	rice vinegar
1	red onion, thinly sliced	2 tbsp.	vegetable oil
1 tbsp.	chopped fresh cilantro	1 tbsp.	finely chopped garlic
		2 tsp.	sugar
		1 tsp.	finely chopped fresh ginger
			Salt and pepper

1. Cut the mango into batons about ½-inch thick and 3 inches long. Place in a large bowl. Add the red pepper, green pepper, red onion and cilantro.

2. In a small bowl whisk together the Fiery Thai Dipping Sauce, rice vinegar, vegetable oil, garlic, sugar and ginger.

3. Pour the dressing over the mango mixture and season to taste with salt and pepper. Toss well.

4. Chill and serve.

SERVES 6

Grilled Zucchini Salad with Roasted Tomato Vinaigrette

Be careful not to over-grill the zucchini or it will turn mushy and brown.

VINAIGRETTE			
6	plum tomatoes	4	zucchini, sliced diagonally ½-inch thick
3 tbsp.	roasted garlic olive oil	1	large sweet onion, sliced
2 tbsp.	balsamic vinegar	2 tbsp.	balsamic vinegar
1 tbsp.	chopped garlic	2 tbsp.	roasted garlic olive oil
1 tbsp.	chopped fresh oregano	¼ cup	chopped fresh basil
	Salt and pepper	2 tbsp.	grated Parmesan cheese

1. Preheat grill to medium-high.

2. Place the tomatoes on the grill. Reduce heat to medium and roast tomatoes, turning occasionally, for 10 to 15 minutes or until charred and tender. Be careful when turning the tomatoes, as they will be soft. Do not turn off the grill.

3. Let cool. Remove and discard skin.

4. Place the tomatoes in a food processor. Add the oil, vinegar, garlic and oregano. Pulse until smooth. Season to taste with salt and pepper. Set vinaigrette aside.

5. In a large bowl toss together the zucchini and onion. Add the balsamic vinegar, oil and salt and pepper to taste. Mix thoroughly. Place zucchini mixture in a grill basket.

6. Grill for 10 to 15 minutes or until the zucchini and onions are tender and slightly charred.

7. Transfer vegetables to a large bowl. Add vinaigrette, toss well and season to taste. Garnish with basil and Parmesan cheese.

SERVES 8

Grilled Bread Salad with Gorgonzola

If you can't find creamy Gorgonzola blue cheese use Cambazola or Roquefort.

1 loaf	crusty Italian white bread		1	roasted red bell pepper, diced
4 tbsp.	balsamic vinegar		1	roasted yellow bell pepper, diced
3 tbsp. +			1 bunch	arugula, washed and patted dry
¼ cup	roasted garlic olive oil		1 cup	crumbled Gorgonzola
	Salt and pepper		2 tbsp.	chopped fresh basil
1	red onion, diced			

1. Slice the bread in half lengthwise.

2. Mix together 2 tbsp. of the vinegar and 3 tbsp. of the oil. Season to taste with salt and pepper. Brush liberally onto the cut sides of the bread. Let marinate for 15 minutes.

3. In a large bowl toss together the red onion, red pepper, yellow pepper, arugula, Gorgonzola and basil. Set aside.

4. Preheat grill to medium-high.

5. Grill the bread, turning once, until lightly browned all over and crisp. Cut the bread into 1-inch cubes and add to the salad.

6. Add the remaining ¼ cup of oil and 2 tbsp. vinegar. Season with salt and pepper and toss thoroughly.

7. Serve immediately.

SERVES 8

Spicy Grilled Vegetable Salad with Smoked Chipotle Dressing

Chipotle chilies are smoked jalapeño peppers. You can find them dried or wet in cans. If you're using dried chipotle chilies, soak them in warm water for 1 to 2 hours beforehand.

1	large red onion, sliced	**DRESSING**	
2	zucchini, thinly sliced	2 to 3	chipotle chilies, puréed
8	large mushrooms, quartered	¾ cup	olive oil
1	red bell pepper, sliced	½ cup	cider vinegar
1	yellow bell pepper, sliced	¼ cup	honey
1	orange bell pepper, sliced	2 tbsp.	chopped fresh cilantro
1 bunch	asparagus cut into 2-inch pieces	1 tsp.	ground cumin
2 tbsp.	olive oil	1 tsp.	salt
1 tbsp.	Bone Dust BBQ Spice (page 97)	2	limes, juiced
1 tbsp.	chopped fresh cilantro		
	Salt and pepper		

1. In a large bowl toss all of the vegetables together. Season with oil and BBQ spice. Toss. Place in a grill basket.

2. Preheat grill to medium-high.

3. To make the dressing, in a food processor combine the chipotle chilies, oil, vinegar, honey, cilantro, cumin, salt and lime juice. Blend until smooth.

4. Grill vegetables for 8 to 10 minutes per side until lightly charred and tender.

5. Transfer vegetables a large bowl. Toss with the dressing and fresh cilantro. Season to taste with salt and pepper.

6. Serve immediately.

SERVES 8

Cucumber and Horseradish Salad

Finely grated fresh horseradish is best in this salad. If you substitute prepared horseradish, make sure to drain it first.

1	English cucumber	2 tbsp.	chopped fresh mint
1	red onion, thinly sliced	2 tbsp.	lemon juice
½ cup	grated fresh horseradish	1 tsp.	ground cumin
3 tbsp.	olive oil		Salt and pepper

1. Cut the cucumber in half lengthwise. Thinly slice the cucumber halves.

2. In a large bowl toss together the cucumber, onion, horseradish, oil, mint, lemon juice and cumin. Season to taste with salt and pepper.

3. Chill and serve.

SERVES 6 TO 8

Grilled Leek and Shrimp Salad

Make sure you wash the leeks really well to get all the grit and sand out of them.

VINAIGRETTE			
⅓ cup	olive oil	4	large leeks, cut in half lengthwise
¼ cup	rice wine vinegar	1	large red onion, sliced
2 tbsp.	chopped fresh cilantro	1	red bell pepper, cubed
1 tbsp.	chopped fresh ginger	1	yellow bell pepper, cubed
1 tbsp.	Dijon mustard	1 lb.	large shrimp, peeled and deveined
2	green onions, finely chopped	2 tbsp.	olive oil
	Salt and pepper	2 tbsp.	rice wine vinegar
		1 tsp.	ground cumin
		1 tsp.	crushed chilies

1. Preheat grill to high.

2. To make the vinaigrette, whisk together the oil, vinegar, cilantro, ginger, mustard, green onions and salt and pepper to taste. Set aside.

3. Cut the leeks into 2-inch chunks and place in a large bowl. Add the red onion, red and yellow peppers, shrimp, olive oil, vinegar, cumin, crushed chilies and salt and pepper to taste. Gently toss to mix thoroughly. Place mixture in a grill basket.

4. Grill vegetables and shrimp for 4 to 5 minutes per side or until tender and slightly charred.

5. Carefully arrange vegetables and shrimp on a serving platter. Pour vinaigrette over top and serve.

SERVES 6 TO 8

Sesame Shrimp and Snap Pea Salad

This is a very simple salad recipe. I like to use the best-quality sesame oil and rice vinegar that I can find.

1 lb.	jumbo shrimp (21–30 per lb.), peeled and deveined	3 tbsp.	rice wine vinegar
2 tbsp.	salt	2 tbsp.	chopped fresh cilantro
6 cups	water	2 tbsp.	dark Asian sesame oil
1	lemon, sliced	1 tbsp.	black sesame seeds
1 lb.	sugar snap peas	1 tbsp.	toasted white sesame seeds
1 cup	sliced radishes		Sea salt

1. Toss the shrimp with 2 tbsp. salt. Let stand for 15 minutes and then rinse under cold running water.

2. Bring 6 cups of water to a rolling boil. Add sliced lemon and shrimp; cook for 3 to 4 minutes or until the shrimp are opaque and just cooked through. Drain and rinse under cold running water until the shrimp are cool. Drain again.

3. Discard any sugar snap peas that are not perfect. Remove the stem end and the string from each pod.

4. In a bowl toss together the shrimp, sugar snap peas, radishes, vinegar, cilantro, sesame oil and black and white sesame seeds.

5. Season to taste with sea salt and serve.

SERVES 6 TO 8

Grilled Portobello Mushroom Salad

Hearty, meaty-textured Portobello mushrooms are one of my favourite vegetables — or fungi — to grill.
They're as good as a steak.

8	large Portobello mushrooms, stems removed	1 tbsp.	coarsely ground black pepper
		1 tbsp.	chopped fresh cilantro
4 cups	hot water	1 tbsp.	sesame seeds
1 tsp.	salt	1 tbsp.	grainy mustard
½ cup	honey	1 tsp.	dark Asian sesame oil
½ cup	hoisin sauce		Salt
¼ cup	soy sauce	3 bunches	arugula
¼ cup	rice vinegar	½ cup	crumbled goat cheese

1. Brush the mushroom caps with a damp cloth to remove any dirt. Place mushrooms in a large bowl. Dissolve salt in hot water and pour over the mushrooms, submerging the mushroom caps so the gills fill with water. Cover with plastic wrap and let the mushrooms steep for 15 minutes.

2. Meanwhile, in a bowl whisk together the honey, hoisin sauce, soy sauce, vinegar, pepper, cilantro, sesame seeds, mustard and sesame oil. Season to taste with salt.

3. Drain mushroom caps and pat dry with paper towels. Place mushroom caps gill side up in a glass dish. Pour honey-hoisin marinade over mushroom caps and let marinate for 2 hours.

4. Preheat grill to medium-high.

5. Remove mushroom caps from marinade, reserving marinade for basting. Place mushrooms gill side up on grill. Grill for 4 to 5 minutes per side, basting frequently with reserved marinade.

6. Remove mushrooms from grill and let stand for 3 minutes to slightly cool and set. Thinly slice mushrooms and serve each cap over a bed of arugula. Garnish with crumbled goat cheese.

SERVES 8

Marinated Mushroom Salad with Curried Raspberry Vinaigrette

Pouring a warm dressing over the mushrooms tenderizes them.

1 lb.	button mushrooms, cleaned and quartered if large	1 bunch	green onions, thinly sliced
½ lb.	oyster mushrooms, cleaned and torn	2	red bell peppers, thinly sliced
½ lb.	cremini mushrooms, cleaned and quartered if large	1 tbsp.	chopped fresh rosemary
		4 cloves	garlic, chopped
½ lb.	shiitake mushrooms, cleaned and thinly sliced	½ cup	vegetable oil
		¼ cup	raspberry vinegar
1	large red onion, diced	1 tbsp.	sugar
		1 tsp.	curry powder
			Salt and pepper

1. In a large bowl combine the mushrooms, red onion, green onions, red peppers, rosemary and garlic.

2. In a small saucepan mix the oil, raspberry vinegar, sugar and curry powder. Slowly heat the dressing, stirring, but do not let it boil.

3. Pour hot dressing over mushroom mixture and toss gently. Season to taste with salt and pepper.

4. Cover and let the mushrooms marinate for 4 hours until tender. Adjust seasoning, gently mix and serve.

SERVES 6 TO 8

Singapore Noodle Salad

You can find Singapore noodles in Asian markets and specialty food stores. Look for a yellow spaghetti-like (but wider) egg noodle.

1 lb.	Singapore noodles
½ lb.	barbecued pork, shredded
1	red onion, thinly sliced
6	green onions, thinly sliced
1	green bell pepper, thinly sliced
1	red bell pepper, thinly sliced
2	oranges, peeled and cut in segments
¼ cup	vegetable oil
¼ cup	orange juice
2 tbsp.	soy sauce
1 tbsp.	chopped fresh cilantro
1 tsp.	curry powder
1 tsp.	sesame oil
1 tsp.	Asian hot sauce
	Salt and pepper to taste

1. Cook noodles according to package instructions. Drain, cool under cold running water and drain again.

2. In a large bowl combine the noodles, pork, red onion, green onions, green and red peppers, orange segments, vegetable oil, orange juice, soy sauce, cilantro, curry powder, sesame oil, hot sauce, salt and pepper. Toss well and serve.

SERVES 6 TO 8

Ruby Red Cabbage Slaw

Don't make this salad too far in advance or it will lose its brilliant red colour.

1	small red cabbage, thinly sliced
½ cup	vegetable oil
¼ cup	cider vinegar
1 tbsp.	mustard seeds
1 tbsp.	brown sugar
1 tsp.	mustard powder
	Salt and pepper
1	red onion, thinly sliced
4	green onions, thinly sliced
2	Granny Smith apples, thinly sliced
1 tbsp.	chopped fresh parsley
1 tbsp.	chopped fresh thyme
1 tsp.	toasted caraway seeds

1. In a large bowl mix together the cabbage, oil, vinegar, mustard seeds, brown sugar, mustard powder and salt and pepper to taste. Mix thoroughly. Cover and let marinate for 2 hours or until the cabbage is tender.

2. Add the red onion, green onions, apples, parsley, thyme and caraway seeds. Toss well, adjust seasoning and serve.

SERVES 8

Memphis-Style Creamy Coleslaw

I have spent a fair amount of time in Memphis, the mecca of ribs in the South. Nothing goes better with ribs or BBQ than a creamy coleslaw. It is almost traditional.

½	green cabbage, very finely sliced
2	large carrots, grated
1	onion, finely chopped
3	green onions, chopped
2 tbsp.	sugar
1 tbsp.	white vinegar
½ tsp.	salt
½ cup	mayonnaise
2 tsp.	mustard powder
1 tsp.	black pepper
¼ tsp.	cayenne pepper

1. In a large bowl combine the cabbage, carrots, onion, green onions, sugar, vinegar and salt. Let marinate for 1 to 2 hours, tossing occasionally.

2. Mix in the mayonnaise, mustard powder, black pepper and cayenne.

3. Refrigerate until ready to serve.

SERVES 8

Firecracker Coleslaw

A rainbow of colours makes this coleslaw festive.

1	small white cabbage, thinly sliced
2	carrots, grated
1	red onion, sliced
1	large red bell pepper, julienned
1	large green bell pepper, julienned
1	large yellow bell pepper, julienned
1	large orange bell pepper, julienned
1 bunch	green onions, thinly sliced
¼ cup	chopped fresh cilantro
1 cup	Spicy Grilled Jalapeño Dressing (page 17)
	Hot sauce
	Salt and pepper

1. In a large bowl combine the cabbage, carrots, onion, bell peppers, green onions and cilantro.

2. Place jalapeño dressing in a microwave-safe container and heat in a microwave on high for 30 to 45 seconds. Pour warm dressing over cabbage mixture. Season to taste with hot sauce, salt and pepper.

3. Mix thoroughly, chill and serve.

SERVES 8

Cheesy Macaroni Salad

This is a great picnic or cottage party salad. What truly makes it is the variety of cheeses. I like to use strong-flavoured cheeses. Look for the double elbow macaroni known as gemelli. The noodles are larger than regular macaroni and make the presentation of the salad much nicer.

1 lb.	double elbow macaroni (gemelli)	1	carrot, peeled and grated
2 tbsp.	olive oil	½ cup	shredded medium or old yellow
1 cup	mayonnaise		Cheddar cheese
½ cup	sour cream	½ cup	shredded old white
2 tbsp.	white wine vinegar		Cheddar cheese
2 tbsp.	lemon juice	½ cup	shredded Emmenthal cheese
1 tsp.	paprika	¼ cup	grated Parmesan cheese
1 tsp.	ground cumin	¼ cup	chopped fresh parsley
1 tsp.	black pepper	1 tbsp.	chopped fresh dill
1 bunch	green onions, thinly sliced		Salt and pepper
1	red onion, thinly sliced		

1. Cook pasta in a pot of boiling salted water until al dente (just tender). Drain, toss with olive oil and let cool.

2. In a large bowl whisk together the mayonnaise, sour cream, vinegar, lemon juice, paprika, cumin and black pepper. Add pasta, green onions, red onion, carrot, all 4 cheeses, parsley and dill. Mix well. Season to taste with salt and pepper.

3. Cover and refrigerate for 1 to 2 hours before serving.

SERVES 8

Chicken Yakitori with Green Onion and Maple Hoisin Glaze

In 1989 I began work at the newly opened SkyDome Hotel in Toronto. With thousands of meals being served daily out of 14 kitchens, I quickly learned a great deal about cooking for big numbers. In the SkyDome Windows Restaurant, a chef named Torichi made hundreds of delectable chicken, beef, shrimp and pork satays for every event. Here is my version of Torichi's little skewers.

4	boneless skinless chicken breasts (each 6 oz.)	**MAPLE HOISIN GLAZE**	
¼ cup	rice wine vinegar	¼ cup	maple syrup
2 tbsp.	soy sauce	¼ cup	hoisin sauce
1 tbsp.	sesame oil	¼ cup	orange juice
1 tbsp.	chopped fresh ginger	1 tbsp.	chopped fresh cilantro
1 tbsp.	chopped garlic	4	green onions, thinly sliced
1 tsp.	curry powder	2 tsp.	sesame seeds
1 tsp.	ground black pepper		Salt and pepper

1. Soak twenty-four 8-inch bamboo skewers in warm water for 1 hour.

2. Slice each chicken breast lengthwise into 6 thin strips, about 1 oz. each. Carefully thread 1 strip of chicken onto one end of each skewer.

3. In a glass dish large enough to hold the chicken skewers, whisk together the vinegar, soy sauce, sesame oil, ginger, garlic, curry powder and pepper. Add the chicken, turning to coat. Marinate chicken, covered and refrigerated, for 4 hours.

4. Preheat grill to medium-high.

5. To make the glaze, in a bowl whisk together the maple syrup, hoisin sauce, orange juice, cilantro, green onions and sesame seeds. Season to taste with salt and pepper.

6. Remove chicken skewers from marinade, discarding marinade. Grill skewers, basting with maple hoisin glaze, for 2 to 3 minutes per side or until chicken is fully cooked. Serve with leftover glaze as a dip.

MAKES 24 SKEWERS

Grilled Spicy Buffalo Wings with Blue Cheese Dressing

When I was a college student we often spent Friday and Saturday nights in Buffalo nightclubs, eating crispy fried wings and guzzling cold beer.

3 lb.	jumbo chicken wings (about 36)	½ cup	Hell's Fire Chili Paste (page 99)
½ cup	Durkee Hot Sauce or	¼ cup	lemon juice
	Franks Redhot Hot Sauce		Salt to taste

1. Trim wing tips from wings and cut through the joint to separate the winglet from the drummette. Place wing pieces in a large bowl and toss with hot sauce, Hell's Fire Chili Paste and lemon juice. Season with salt.

2. Cover, refrigerate and marinate for 24 hours.

3. Preheat grill to medium.

4. Remove chicken wings from marinade and place in a grill basket.

5. Grill wings for 10 to 12 minutes per side, turning every 5 to 6 minutes, or until fully cooked, golden brown and crisp.

6. Carefully remove from grill basket and serve with Chunky Blue Cheese Dressing (page 13).

SERVES 4

Margarita Wings

Wings and beer are a great combination, but I especially like the way tequila and wings work together. Besides, a few shots of tequila always make cooking a little easier — and tastier.

3 lb.	jumbo chicken wings (about 36)	**MARGARITA WING SAUCE**	
3 tbsp.	lemon pepper	1 cup	honey
3 tbsp.	vegetable oil	¾ cup	prepared mustard
		½ cup	lime juice
		¼ cup	gold tequila
		3 tbsp.	chopped fresh cilantro
		2 tbsp.	hot sauce

1. Preheat grill to medium.

2. Trim wing tips from wings and cut through the joint to separate the winglet from the drummette. Place wing pieces in a large bowl and toss with lemon pepper and vegetable oil.

3. To make the margarita wing sauce, in a large bowl whisk together the honey, mustard, lime juice, tequila, cilantro and hot sauce. Set aside.

4. Place seasoned chicken wings in a grill basket.

5. Grill wings for 10 to 12 minutes per side, turning every 5 to 6 minutes, or until fully cooked, golden brown and crisp.

6. Carefully remove wings from grill basket and add to margarita wing sauce. Toss well and serve.

SERVES 4

Infiniti Dip

You have probably heard of seven-layer dip and nine-layer dip. Well, here's one called Infiniti Dip. I developed this recipe for the crew of Patrick Racing. It started out as seven layers and just kept on growing. The deeper the dish you use, the more layers you can create. It's a little over the top, but so am I.

You will need to do a little bit of basic preparation before you start assembling the layered dip. You could buy premade salsa and guacamole, but I prefer to make my own.

Guacamole

2	avocados, peeled and seeded	2 cloves	garlic, minced
3 tbsp.	lemon juice	3	green onions, finely chopped
1 tbsp.	chopped fresh cilantro		Hot sauce, salt and black pepper
½	small red onion, diced		

1. In a bowl mash the avocados with a fork. Stir in the lemon juice, cilantro, onion, garlic and green onions.

2. Season to taste with hot sauce, salt and pepper. Cover and refrigerate.

MAKES ABOUT 2 CUPS

Fire-Roasted Four-Pepper Salsa

2	red bell peppers, halved and seeded	2 tbsp.	olive oil
		2 to 3	smoked chipotle chilies in adobo sauce, puréed
1	yellow bell pepper, halved and seeded	1 tbsp.	chopped garlic
		1 tbsp.	chopped fresh cilantro
1	green bell pepper, halved and seeded	1 tbsp.	lime juice
			Salt and coarsely ground black pepper to taste
1	red onion, peeled and quartered		

1. Preheat grill to high.

2. On a lightly greased grill, roast the red, yellow and green peppers and the red onion until charred all over and tender.

3. Peel any loose skin from the peppers. Dice the peppers and onion; place in a large bowl.

4. Add the olive oil, puréed chipotle chilies, garlic, cilantro, lime juice, salt and pepper. Mix thoroughly, cover and refrigerate at least 1 hour.

MAKES 2 TO 3 CUPS

Salsa Verde

Also known as Green Salsa, this salsa is made from roasted poblano chili peppers and tomatillos. The tomatillo is a fruit that looks like a small green tomato. If you can't find tomatillos, substitute green tomatoes.

6	tomatillos, chopped	4	green onions, finely chopped
2	poblano peppers, roasted, peeled, seeded and diced	¼ cup	chopped fresh cilantro
2	jalapeño peppers, seeded and finely chopped	2 tbsp.	white vinegar
		2 tbsp.	olive oil
1	small yellow onion, finely diced	Pinch	ground cumin
4 cloves	garlic, minced		Salt and pepper

1. In a bowl mix the tomatillos, poblano and jalapeño peppers, onion, garlic, green onions, cilantro, vinegar and olive oil. Season to taste with cumin, salt and pepper.

MAKES ABOUT 2 CUPS

Continued ...

OTHER NEEDS			
8	plum tomatoes, finely chopped	2 cups	shredded yellow Cheddar cheese
1	red onion, diced	2 cups	shredded Monterey Jack cheese
1 bunch	green onions, finely chopped	2	jars (each 450 mL)
1	jar (12 oz.) pickled sliced		Chili Con Queso Cheese Sauce
	jalapeño peppers	2 cups	shredded spicy Pepper Jack cheese
1 cup	sliced pitted black olives	1	tub (500 mL) sour cream
1 cup	bacon bits	2 cups	shredded mozzarella cheese
¼ cup	chopped fresh cilantro	1 cup	Hickory Sticks Smoked Flavour potato
1	can (19 oz.) refried beans		matchsticks

1. Prepare the Guacamole, Fire-Roasted Four-Pepper Salsa and the Salsa Verde.

2. In a bowl mix the tomatoes, red onion, green onions, pickled jalapeños, olives, bacon bits and cilantro. Set aside.

3. To assemble the Infiniti Dip, spread even layers of the ingredients in a 6-inch-deep glass casserole dish in the following order:

Layer 1   all the refried beans
Layer 2   half of the Fire-Roasted Four-Pepper Salsa
Layer 3   1 cup of the Cheddar cheese
Layer 4   half of the Guacamole
Layer 5   1 cup of the Monterey Jack cheese
Layer 6   1 jar of the Chili Con Queso Cheese Sauce
Layer 7   half of the Salsa Verde
Layer 8   1 cup of the spicy Pepper Jack cheese
Layer 9   half of the sour cream
Layer 10   1 cup of the mozzarella cheese
Layer 11   rest of the Fire-Roasted Four-Pepper Salsa
Layer 12   1 cup of the Cheddar cheese
Layer 13   rest of the Guacamole

Layer 14	1 cup of the Monterey Jack cheese
Layer 15	the second jar of the Chili Con Queso Cheese Sauce
Layer 16	rest of the Salsa Verde
Layer 17	1 cup of the spicy Pepper Jack cheese
Layer 18	half of the sour cream
Layer 19	1 cup of the mozzarella cheese
Layers 20–26	all of the tomato/green onion/olive mixture

4. Cover with plastic wrap and refrigerate for 2 hours to allow the dip to set.

5. To serve, garnish the top of the dip with Layer 27, the Hickory Sticks.

6. Serve with tortilla chips.

SERVES 8 TO 12

Cinnamon-Skewered Lamb Kebabs with Coconut Chili Chutney

While on a recent trip to India I came across a coconut chutney that was superb, a blend of freshly grated coconut and hot chili peppers. It's a great accompaniment to lamb or chicken.

16	5-inch cinnamon sticks	1 tbsp.	minced ginger
2 lb.	boneless leg of lamb	1 tsp.	salt
¼ cup	vegetable oil	½ tsp.	ground cinnamon
¼ cup	rice vinegar	4 cloves	garlic, minced
2 tbsp.	curry powder	1	red chili pepper, minced
1 tbsp.	chopped fresh cilantro		

Tip

Save your empty coconut shells and use as wood chips on your grill. They add great flavour.

1. Soak the cinnamon sticks in warm water for 1 hour.

2. Trim the lamb of any excess fat. Cut lamb into ½-inch cubes.

3. Skewer about 2 oz. (2 cubes) of lamb onto one end of each cinnamon stick.

4. In a glass dish large enough to hold the kebabs, whisk together the oil, vinegar, curry powder, cilantro, ginger, salt, ground cinnamon, garlic and chili pepper. Add the lamb skewers, turning to coat. Cover and refrigerate for 2 hours to marinate.

5. Preheat grill to medium-high.

6. Remove lamb kebabs from marinade, discarding marinade. Grill for 3 to 4 minutes per side for medium.

7. Serve immediately with Coconut Chili Chutney (recipe follows).

SERVES 8

Coconut Chili Chutney

1	coconut	¼ cup	rice wine vinegar
2 tbsp.	vegetable oil	¼ cup	water
2	green finger chili peppers, sliced	1 tbsp.	sugar
1	red finger chili pepper, sliced	½ tsp.	nutmeg
1	onion, sliced		Salt and pepper
3 cloves	garlic, minced		

1. Hammer an ice pick or screwdriver into the black dots at the end of the coconut; drain and reserve the water. Tap the coconut with the hammer to break it into pieces.

2. Use a vegetable peeler to remove the skin from the coconut meat. Shave the coconut in a food processor. Set aside.

3. Heat the oil in a medium saucepan over high heat. Add the chilies, onion and garlic; sauté, stirring, for 3 to 4 minutes or until tender.

4. Add the shaved coconut; sauté for another 3 to 4 minutes.

5. Add the reserved coconut water, vinegar, water, sugar and nutmeg. Bring to a boil, reduce heat to medium-low and simmer, stirring occasionally, for 10 minutes. Season to taste with salt and pepper.

6. Remove from heat and transfer to a bowl. Cool completely, then cover and refrigerate until needed.

MAKES ABOUT 2 CUPS

Turkish Shish Kebabs with Pomegranate Glaze

Pomegranate molasses, used in the glaze, can be found in specialty food stores and in Middle Eastern markets.

1 lb.	ground lamb	**POMEGRANATE GLAZE**	
2 tbsp.	minced fresh ginger	½ cup	pomegranate molasses
2 tbsp.	chopped fresh cilantro	½ cup	red currant jelly
2 tbsp.	Worcestershire sauce	¼ cup	dry sherry
1 tsp.	black pepper	1 tbsp.	chopped fresh mint
1 tsp.	curry powder	1 tbsp.	olive oil
1 tsp.	cayenne pepper	4 cloves	garlic, minced
½ tsp.	ground cumin		Salt and pepper
½ tsp.	ground coriander		
1	small onion, finely chopped		
4 cloves	garlic, minced		
	Salt		

1. Soak eight 10- to 12-inch bamboo skewers in hot water for 1 hour. (Or use metal skewers.)

2. Preheat grill to medium-high.

3. In a bowl combine the lamb, ginger, cilantro, Worcestershire sauce, black pepper, curry powder, cayenne, cumin, coriander, onion and garlic. Season to taste with salt.

4. Divide into 8 equal-sized portions. Moisten your hands with cold water and knead each portion to ensure that each is fully mixed with the spices. Mould each portion around each skewer, shaping it into a uniform sausage about 6 inches long.

5. To make the pomegranate glaze, combine the molasses, red currant jelly, sherry, mint, oil and garlic. Season to taste with salt and pepper.

6. Grill kebabs for 8 to 10 minutes, turning every couple of minutes and basting with pomegranate glaze, until golden brown but still juicy and pink inside.

7. Serve with remaining glaze.

MAKES 8 KEBABS

Lobster-Stuffed Devilled Eggs

What can I say except it's devilishly good.

12	extra-large eggs	1 tsp.	Bone Dust BBQ Spice (page 97)
½ cup	mayonnaise	Dash	hot sauce
1 tbsp.	chopped fresh dill	½ lb.	lobster meat (fresh or frozen)
1 tbsp.	Dijon mustard		Salt and pepper
1 tbsp.	lemon juice		Sprigs of fresh dill

1. Place the eggs in a large pot and cover with cold water. Bring to a boil over high heat. Cover the pan and remove from the heat. Let stand 15 minutes.

2. Drain the eggs and run under cold water for 15 minutes.

3. Peel the eggs, being careful not to break the whites.

4. Using a sharp knife cut the eggs in half lengthwise.

5. With a small spoon, carefully remove the yolk and place in a bowl.

6. Arrange the whites on a cookie sheet lined with paper towel.

7. Mash the yolks. The best way to do this is to press them through a fine sieve. If you do not have one, just mash them with a fork.

8. Mix in the mayonnaise, dill, mustard, lemon juice, BBQ spice and hot sauce.

9. Pick through the lobster meat to make sure there are no bits of shell. Break the lobster meat into very small pieces and add to the egg mixture. Gently mix the eggs and lobster together to make a sticky mass. Season to taste with salt and pepper.

10. Spoon the lobster mixture into each of the egg whites. Pile it high, as these are killer eggs.

11. Garnish with sprigs of dill.

MAKES 24 YUMMY EGGS

Grilled Oysters Stuffed with Snow Crab and Bacon in a Mango BBQ Sauce

I served this recipe at the Taste of CART event at the Mid Ohio Race Course in August 2000. It was one of three recipes that helped me win the CART Best Chef Competition.

½ lb.	snow crab meat, thawed and drained	1 tbsp.	lemon juice
		Dash	hot sauce
6 slices	bacon, cooked crisp and diced		Salt and pepper
2 cloves	garlic, minced	16	oysters
1	small onion, finely chopped	1	mango, peeled and pitted
1 tbsp.	chopped fresh dill	½ cup	BBQ sauce

---

1. Preheat grill to medium-high.

2. In a bowl mix together the crab meat, bacon, garlic, onion, dill and lemon juice. Season to taste with hot sauce, salt and pepper.

3. Using an oyster knife, shuck the oysters over a bowl. Strain the liquor into the crab mixture.

4. Remove the oysters from their shells and set aside. Place 1 heaping tablespoon of crab mixture in each of 16 half shells. Top each with an oyster.

5. In a food processor purée the mango until smooth. Add the BBQ sauce and blend until incorporated.

6. Place the stuffed oysters on a grill screen. Top each oyster with 1 tbsp. mango sauce. Place on the grill, close the lid and cook for 10 to 12 minutes or until the mango sauce and stuffing are hot.

7. Carefully remove from the grill and serve.

SERVES 4

Never Lose Clams Casino

I love clams, whether raw on the half shell or steamed, but what I like most is baked clams. My version of the classic Clams Casino uses lots of cheese and smoky bacon. When buying clams (a.k.a. qua-hogs), choose large hard-shell Atlantic clams such as cherrystone, littleneck or topneck.

12	large cherrystone or littleneck clams	1 tbsp.	chopped fresh parsley
			Salt and pepper
4 slices	bacon, diced	½ cup	grated Parmesan cheese
2 cloves	garlic, minced	½ cup	shredded mozzarella cheese
¼ cup	finely chopped onion	¼ cup	shredded Swiss cheese
½	red bell pepper, finely chopped	¼ cup	dry bread crumbs
½ cup	tomato sauce		

1. Using an oyster knife, shuck the clams and set aside in the refrigerator for later.

2. In a frying pan over medium-high heat, cook the bacon for 3 to 5 minutes or until just crisp. Drain off all but 2 tbsp. of bacon fat.

3. Add the garlic, onion and red pepper; sauté for 3 to 5 minutes or until tender. Stir in tomato sauce and parsley; quickly bring to a boil. Remove from heat and season to taste with salt and pepper. Let cool slightly.

4. In a bowl mix together the Parmesan cheese, mozzarella cheese, Swiss cheese and bread crumbs.

5. Preheat oven to 425°F.

6. Spread a layer of coarse salt on a baking sheet. Put the clams back in the shells and arrange them evenly on the baking sheet.

7. Place 1 tbsp. of the bacon-onion mixture on top of each clam, and then top each clam with the cheese and bread crumb mixture.

8. Bake clams for 8 to 10 minutes or until the cheese is melted and golden brown.

9. Let rest for 3 minutes before serving.

SERVES 6

Mustard Leaf Steam-Grilled Mussels with Dijon Cream Sauce

If you can't find mustard leaves, use pine needles, seaweed or collard greens.

2 bunches	large mustard greens	4 cloves	garlic, minced
2 lb.	blue mussels, bearded and rinsed	¼ cup	dry sherry
2 tbsp.	sea salt	¼ cup	Dijon mustard
2 tbsp.	mustard seeds	1 tbsp.	grainy mustard
2 tbsp.	chopped fresh thyme	1 cup	whipping cream
2 tbsp.	butter		Salt and freshly ground
2	large shallots, sliced		black pepper to taste

1. Wash the mustard greens to remove any dirt, then soak leaves in cold water for 15 minutes.

2. In a large bowl toss the mussels with salt, mustard seeds and thyme. Set aside.

3. In a small saucepan over medium-high heat, melt the butter. Sauté the shallots and garlic for 3 minutes or until translucent. Add the sherry, Dijon mustard and grainy mustard; bring to a boil. Add the cream and return to a boil. Reduce heat to medium-low and simmer for 5 minutes or until the sauce evenly coats the back of a wooden spoon. Remove from heat, season with salt and pepper, and keep warm.

4. Preheat grill to high.

5. Working quickly, lay half of the mustard leaves on the grill. Add the seasoned mussels and cover with the remaining mustard leaves. Close the lid and let the mussels steam-grill for 10 to 12 minutes or until the mussels open.

6. Carefully remove and discard the top mustard leaves. Transfer mussels to a large bowl (discard any that have not opened). Add the Dijon cream sauce, toss, and serve with a fresh baguette.

SERVES 4

Rosemary-Skewered Salmon Satays with Honey Tangerine Glaze

When buying rosemary for this recipe look for long, large branches with stems thick enough to be able to support the weight of the salmon.

8	thick rosemary branches (each about 6 inches long)	
1½ lb.	thick Atlantic salmon fillets, skinned	
3 tbsp.	Licorice Rub (page 103)	
3 tbsp.	olive oil	

HONEY TANGERINE GLAZE

¼ cup	honey
¼ cup	orange marmalade
¼ cup	Cointreau or Grand Marnier
¼ cup	tangerine or orange juice
1 tbsp.	chopped fresh mint
½ tsp.	cayenne pepper
	Salt and pepper

1. Soak the rosemary branches in warm water for 1 hour.

2. Cut the salmon into twenty-four 1½-inch cubes; place in a bowl. Add Licorice Rub and olive oil; toss well.

3. Thread 3 cubes of salmon onto each rosemary branch and place in a glass dish to marinate for 20 minutes.

4. Meanwhile, prepare the glaze by combining the honey, marmalade, Cointreau, tangerine juice, mint and cayenne in a small saucepan. Over low heat, stir constantly until thoroughly mixed and smooth. Remove from heat and season to taste with salt and pepper.

5. Preheat grill to medium-high.

6. Grill salmon skewers for 2 to 3 minutes per side, basting with honey tangerine glaze. Serve immediately with remaining glaze for dipping.

SERVES 4

Shrimp Parfait with Lucifer Cocktail Sauce

Shrimp cocktail has to be one of my favourite dishes. The best I've ever had comes from St. Elmo Steakhouse in Indianapolis. Their shrimp cocktail is known for its serious kick of fresh horseradish — sinus burner for sure.

My only complaint about restaurant shrimp cocktails is that there is never enough shrimp. My own recipe solves that problem. It's not cheap, but it is certainly delicious.

Lucifer Cocktail Sauce

½ cup	freshly grated horseradish	1 tbsp.	white vinegar
½ cup	ketchup	2 tsp.	hot sauce
½ cup	chili sauce		Salt and pepper to taste
2 tbsp.	lemon juice		

1. In a small bowl stir together the horseradish, ketchup, chili sauce, lemon juice, vinegar, hot sauce, salt and pepper. Refrigerate until ready to serve.

MAKES ABOUT 2 CUPS

Crab Salad

1 lb.	crab meat	1 tbsp.	lemon juice
½	small red onion, diced	1 tbsp.	grainy mustard
¼ cup	mayonnaise	Dash	hot sauce
1 tbsp.	chopped fresh dill		Salt and pepper to taste

1. In a bowl stir together the crab meat, onion, mayonnaise, dill, lemon juice, mustard, hot sauce, salt and pepper. Refrigerate until needed.

MAKES ABOUT 2 CUPS

Shrimp Halves

6 cups	water	2 tsp.	salt
¼ cup	lemon juice	2 lb.	large shrimp (21–30 per lb.),
2 sprigs	fresh dill		peeled and deveined
8	peppercorns		

1. In a large saucepan bring the water to a boil. Add the lemon juice, dill, peppercorns and salt; return to a boil.

2. Add shrimp; cook for 3 to 4 minutes or until the shrimp are opaque and just cooked through. Drain and rinse under cold water until cool. Drain again.

3. With a sharp knife slice each shrimp in half lengthwise.

4. Cover and refrigerate until needed.

Grilled Tiger Shrimp

20	jumbo tiger shrimp, peeled and deveined, tails left on	3 tbsp.	olive oil
3 tbsp.	Bay Seasoning (page 98)	1	lime, juiced
		Special equipment: 4 semi-circular metal skewers	

Continued...

1. In a bowl toss the shrimp with Bay Seasoning, olive oil and lime juice. Marinate for 30 minutes.

2. Thread 5 shrimp onto each skewer. Cover and refrigerate until needed.

The Parfait

Fire-Roasted Four-Pepper Salsa (page 40)	**4 sprigs**	**fresh dill**
Guacamole (page 40)	**4**	**lemon wedges**

1. Place a large spoonful of crab salad into each of 4 large parfait or milkshake glasses.

2. Onto this spoon a little Fire-Roasted Four-Pepper Salsa. Top with a dollop of guacamole.

3. Layer 6 to 8 shrimp halves in each glass and top with a dollop of cocktail sauce.

4. Repeat this layering until you reach the top of the glass, ending with a layer of shrimp halves. Refrigerate for 1 hour.

5. Preheat grill to medium-high.

6. Grill skewered jumbo shrimp for 2 to 3 minutes per side or until opaque and just cooked through.

7. Garnish each parfait with a dill sprig and lemon wedge. Balance a skewer of shrimp on top of each parfait.

8. Serve immediately.

SERVES 4

Bacon-Wrapped Scallops with Maple Chili Glaze

Atlantic scallops are a real treat, especially those from the cold waters of the Bay of Fundy. My mom and dad had their honeymoon in Digby, Nova Scotia, Canada's most famous scallop town. On one of my excursions I had some delicious bacon-wrapped scallops glazed with maple syrup. Here's my version.

8 slices	thick bacon		1 tbsp.	chopped fresh dill
16	fresh jumbo scallops, trimmed of muscle		1 tbsp.	sambal chili paste
			1 tbsp.	olive oil
1 tbsp.	Bone Dust BBQ Spice (page 97)		2	green onions, finely chopped
¼ cup	maple syrup			Salt and pepper to taste
¼ cup	orange juice			

1. Soak sixteen 6-inch bamboo skewers in hot water for 30 minutes.

2. Fry the bacon until it is just starting to get crispy, about halfway done. Drain on paper towels and cut each slice in half.

3. Drain the scallops well and pat dry with paper towels.

4. Sprinkle the scallops with BBQ spice. Wrap each scallop with a half slice of bacon.

5. Skewer 1 scallop (running the skewer through the bacon and scallop) onto one end of each skewer. Set aside.

6. In a bowl whisk together the maple syrup, orange juice, dill, sambal, oil, green onions, salt and pepper.

7. Preheat grill to medium-high.

8. Place scallops on a grill screen and grill for 3 to 4 minutes per side, basting liberally with the maple chili basting sauce, or until the bacon is crisp and the scallops are just done. Be careful not to overcook.

9. Serve with remaining basting sauce.

MAKES 16 SKEWERS

Tandoori Jumbo Prawns

We were sailing in the backwaters of the Indian Ocean outside Cochin, India. It was dark, and I was wet from a tropical rainstorm. The clouds parted as we docked on the shore of the canal. The open grill with spurting hot coals fired back up. Dinner was moments away. Red snapper fillets, grouper steaks and the largest prawns I had ever seen, marinated in tandoori spices and waiting to be grilled. The host chef invited me to join his staff on the grill to prepare this seafood feast. I jumped at the opportunity. Here is the recipe.

¾ cup	lemon juice	**TANDOORI SAUCE**	
¼ cup	chopped fresh ginger	¾ cup	plain yogurt
1 tbsp.	red chili powder	¼ cup	whipping cream
1 tsp.	salt	2 tbsp.	chopped fresh ginger
8 cloves	garlic, minced	1 tsp.	turmeric
24	jumbo prawns (5–6 per lb.),	1 tsp.	red chili powder
	peeled and deveined,	1 tsp.	ground white pepper
	tails left on	1 tsp.	garam masala
½ cup	melted butter	8 cloves	garlic, minced

1. In a large, shallow dish whisk together the lemon juice, ginger, chili powder, salt and garlic. Add the prawns, turning to coat well, and marinate for 20 minutes.

2. Meanwhile, make the tandoori sauce. In a large bowl stir together well the yogurt, cream, ginger, turmeric, chili powder, pepper, garam masala and garlic.

3. Remove prawns from marinade, discarding marinade, and add to the tandoori sauce. Gently stir to completely coat the prawns. Marinate, covered and refrigerated, for 1 hour.

4. Preheat grill to medium-high.

5. Thread 4 prawns onto each of 6 metal skewers.

6. Grill prawns for 3 to 4 minutes per side, basting with melted butter.

7. Serve immediately.

SERVES 6

Octoberfest Pig's Tails

The Kitchener-Waterloo area hosts the largest Octoberfest celebration outside Germany. Pig's tails are a specialty of the area, with the largest consumption during Octoberfest. Schneider's Meats sells cooked pig's tails in a can with a sweet brown gravy, not a bad product, but I say there is nothing better than your own home cooking. Allow yourself a lot of time to prepare these, as well as a lot of warm wet towels to clean your hands with — this is the stickiest recipe in the book!

3 lb.	fully trimmed and cleaned pig's tails (about 12)	**SWEET-AND-SPICY SAUCE**	
3 bottles	beer	½ cup	brown sugar
6	whole cloves	½ cup	ketchup
8	peppercorns	¼ cup	water
2	bay leaves	2 tbsp.	Worcestershire sauce
	Salt to taste		Salt and pepper

1. Place the pig's tails in a large stockpot. Pour in the beer and add enough water to cover the tails. Add the cloves, peppercorns, bay leaves and salt.

2. Bring to a rolling boil, reduce heat to medium-low and simmer, uncovered, for 2 hours.

3. Preheat oven to 375°F.

4. Remove pig's tails from the pot and set on a lightly greased baking sheet. Discard the cooking liquid. Season tails with salt and roast for 45 minutes, checking periodically that they are not burning.

5. Meanwhile, make the sweet-and-spicy sauce. In a small bowl whisk together the brown sugar, ketchup, water and Worcestershire sauce. Season to taste with salt and pepper.

6. After 45 minutes, baste the pig's tails with the sauce. Roast for another 15 minutes to caramelize. Remove from oven, baste again with sauce and serve immediately with wet cloths.

SERVES 6

Grilled Portobello Mushrooms Stuffed with Smoked Chicken and Oka Cheese

Three of my favourite ingredients brought together in one simple recipe. For the chicken, try my Devil's Brewed Roast Chicken (page 184).

8	large Portobello mushrooms	2 cups	shredded smoked chicken
4 cups	hot water	1½ cups	shredded Oka cheese
¼ cup	olive oil	½ cup	softened cream cheese
¼ cup +		¼ cup	BBQ sauce
1 tbsp.	cider vinegar	1 tbsp.	chopped fresh sage
	Salt and freshly ground	½ cup	dry bread crumbs
	black pepper to taste	½ cup	grated Parmesan cheese
1	small yellow onion, finely diced		

1. Brush any dirt off the mushrooms and cut off and discard the stems. Put the mushroom caps in a large bowl and cover with the hot water; let stand for 10 to 15 minutes to allow the mushrooms to soften. Drain and pat dry on paper towels.

2. In the same bowl, mix together the olive oil, ¼ cup of the cider vinegar, salt and pepper. Add mushroom caps, turning to coat well, and let marinate while you make the stuffing.

3. In a bowl stir together the onion, smoked chicken, Oka cheese, cream cheese, BBQ sauce, sage and remaining 1 tbsp. of vinegar. Season to taste with salt and pepper. Divide the mixture into 8 equal portions and flatten to the size of the mushroom caps.

4. In a small bowl combine the bread crumbs and Parmesan cheese. Set aside.

5. Preheat grill to medium-high. Spray a grill screen with nonstick cooking spray. Place on the grill and preheat for 5 minutes.

6. Grill the mushrooms gill side down for 4 to 5 minutes or until slightly charred and just tender.

7. Turn mushrooms over and place the stuffing mixture on each cap. Top with a liberal dusting of the bread crumb mixture. Close the lid and cook for 7 to 8 more minutes or until the cheese is hot and bubbling and the bread crumbs are golden brown.

8. Serve with mixed greens dressed with Astrida's Lemon Vinaigrette (page 14).

SERVES 8

Grape Leaf-Wrapped Camembert with Bacon and Roasted Onion Topping

When the wrapped Camembert is slowly grilled, the cheese takes on a sweet nutty aroma from the grape leaves.

1	large onion, thinly sliced	1 tbsp.	chopped fresh thyme
2 tbsp.	olive oil		Salt and cracked black pepper
1 tsp.	salt	Dash	cider vinegar
½ tsp.	ground cumin	1	small wheel Camembert (125 g)
½ tsp.	chili powder	4	large grape leaves
8 slices	smoked bacon		Spiced olive oil for basting

1. Preheat oven to 400°F.

2. In an ovenproof dish toss together the onion, oil, salt, cumin and chili powder. Roast, stirring two or three times, for 30 to 40 minutes or until the onions are lightly charred and tender. Let cool.

3. Meanwhile, fry the bacon until crisp. Drain on paper towels and let cool. Crumble the bacon.

4. Chop the roasted onions and mix with the bacon and thyme. Season to taste with salt, pepper and a dash of cider vinegar.

5. Using a butter knife, scrape the white mould off the top of the Camembert. Season with cracked black pepper.

6. Lay the grape leaves in a circle, overlapping slightly. Pat the top of the leaves dry with paper towels.

7. Place the Camembert in the centre of the leaves. Top with the onion mixture and spread it evenly. Wrap the leaves over the Camembert and press firmly to seal. If necessary brush the edge of the leaves with olive oil to help form a seal.

8. Preheat grill to medium-low.

9. Place the wrapped Camembert on the grill onion-topping side up and grill for 8 to 12 minutes or until the cheese is soft. Press gently with a butter knife to check.

10. Remove from grill to a serving plate. Let cool for 2 minutes, then carefully unwrap the leaves from the cheese. Spread or spoon the warm cheese over baguette slices.

SERVES 4

Sultry Sides

Jumbo Stuffed Mushrooms

Buy the largest white mushrooms you can find, with firm white caps. The larger the mushroom, the deeper the cavity to fill with tasty stuffing.

8	**very large field mushrooms**
½ cup	**fresh bread crumbs**
½ cup	**shredded provolone cheese**
¼ cup	**grated Parmesan cheese**
2 tbsp.	**water**
1 tbsp.	**chopped fresh basil**
2 tsp.	**chopped garlic**
6 slices	**double smoked bacon, diced and fried crisp**
	Salt and pepper to taste

1. Preheat grill to medium.

2. Remove stems from the mushrooms and clean the caps. Pat dry.

3. In a bowl stir together the bread crumbs, provolone cheese, Parmesan, water, basil, garlic, bacon, salt and pepper.

4. Fill the mushroom caps with the cheese mixture, gently pressing the mixture into the caps.

5. Place the mushroom caps on the grill. Close the lid and bake for 10 to 15 minutes or until the mushrooms are tender, the stuffing is golden brown and the cheese is melted.

SERVES 8

Senior's Sautéed Mushrooms

Senior's is my favourite steakhouse in Toronto. I sure like the taramosalata and the French blue cheese dressing and the tender garlicky rib steak and the fantastic service. But above all I love their sautéed mushrooms. Owner Eddy Marlet says the key to great sautéed mushrooms is a hot pan and great seasoning. This is my version of his recipe.

¼ cup	**vegetable oil**
1 lb.	**large white mushrooms, quartered**
3 cloves	**garlic, minced**
2 tsp.	**Bone Dust BBQ Spice (page 97)**
	Salt

1. Heat a large frying pan over high heat for 5 minutes. Add the oil and heat until it starts to smoke.

2. Add the mushrooms; sauté for 4 to 5 minutes, stirring occasionally, until golden brown and crisp. Add the garlic; sauté for 1 minute.

3. Add the BBQ spice and season to taste with lots of salt.

4. Serve immediately with your favourite grilled steak.

SERVES 4

Foil-Roasted Shallots, Corn and Shiitake Mushrooms

Wrapping vegetables in foil bundles allows them to steam, staying tender and flavourful.

16	shallots, peeled and halved
4 ears	corn, cut into 1-inch rounds
12	shiitake mushrooms, stems removed, quartered
4 cloves	garlic, thinly sliced
2 tbsp.	cider vinegar
2 tbsp.	melted butter
1 tbsp.	chopped fresh thyme
	Salt and pepper to taste

1. Preheat grill to medium-high.

2. In a bowl toss together the shallots, corn, mushrooms, garlic, thyme, vinegar, butter, salt and pepper.

3. Place mixture in the centre of an 8- x 12-inch sheet of foil. Fold to seal.

4. Place on the grill, close the lid and roast for 20 to 30 minutes or until hot and tender.

5. Serve with Roberto Moreno's Lime Veal Chop (page 161), if desired.

SERVES 8

Foil-Steamed Asparagus with Blue Cheese

I like to use thinner asparagus, which cooks quickly and is tender.

2 lb.	asparagus
4	shallots, finely chopped
1 tbsp.	pink peppercorns
1 tbsp.	chopped fresh thyme
3 tbsp.	butter
2 tbsp.	lemon juice
	Salt to taste
1 cup	crumbled blue cheese

1. Preheat grill to high.

2. Lay two 12-inch-square sheets of foil on top of each other. Pile the asparagus in the centre of the foil. Sprinkle with the shallots, pink peppercorns and thyme. Dollop with butter and drizzle with lemon juice. Fold over and seal the foil.

3. Place the bundle on the grill, close the lid and bake the asparagus for 12 to 15 minutes or until it is tender and hot.

4. Carefully remove the bundle from the grill and open the package. The steam will be hot. Transfer asparagus to a serving platter. Season with salt and garnish with crumbled blue cheese.

SERVES 6 TO 8

Creamed Spinach

I've tried many versions of creamed spinach, but none match my mother's recipe.

1 lb.	fresh spinach	¼ cup	cream cheese
3 tbsp.	butter	1 tbsp.	chopped fresh parsley
1	shallot, diced	¼ tsp.	nutmeg
2 cloves	garlic, minced	Pinch	cinnamon
1 cup	whipping cream		Salt and pepper to taste

1. Remove the woody stems from the spinach. Wash spinach well in cold water. Drain and pat dry with paper towels.

2. Roughly chop the spinach.

3. In a frying pan, melt the butter over medium heat. Sauté the shallot and garlic for 2 to 3 minutes or until translucent and tender. Add the spinach; sauté for 5 minutes or until the spinach is wilted and the water has evaporated from the pan.

4. Add the cream and cream cheese, stirring until smooth. Bring to a boil and reduce liquid, stirring frequently, until the sauce is thick. Season with nutmeg, cinnamon, parsley, salt and pepper.

5. Serve immediately.

SERVES 4

Grilled Parsnips and Carrots with Vanilla Maple Syrup

Before grilling root vegetables, it's best to blanch them in boiling salted water until they are just tender.

1	vanilla bean	2 tbsp.	olive oil
¼ cup	maple syrup	2 tbsp.	balsamic vinegar
3	large carrots, peeled	1 tbsp.	Bone Dust BBQ Spice (page 97)
6	parsnips, peeled	3	green onions, finely chopped
2	sweet onions, peeled and cut into 8 wedges	1 tbsp.	chopped fresh thyme
			Salt and pepper

1. Slice the vanilla bean in half lengthwise and scrape the seeds into a small saucepan. Add the vanilla bean and maple syrup. Heat over medium heat for 5 minutes. Let cool for 1 to 2 hours to allow the flavours to combine. Discard the vanilla bean.

2. Preheat grill to medium-high.

3. Cut the carrots and parsnips into 3-inch lengths. Cut any thick chunks in half lengthwise.

4. Blanch the carrots and parsnips in boiling salted water for 3 to 5 minutes or until just tender. Drain and let cool slightly.

5. In a bowl toss together the carrots, parsnips, onions, olive oil, balsamic vinegar and BBQ spice. Place mixture in a grill basket and grill for 5 to 6 minutes per side or until lightly charred and tender.

6. Carefully remove the vegetables from the basket and in a clean bowl toss with the green onions, thyme and the vanilla maple syrup. Season to taste with salt and pepper.

7. Serve immediately.

SERVES 4 TO 6

Southern Corn and Cheddar Pudding

Canned creamed corn is the secret to making this pudding rich and creamy.

5	eggs	½ tsp.	baking powder
1½ cups	whipping cream	½ tsp.	salt
1 cup	milk	¼ tsp.	black pepper
⅓ cup	all-purpose flour	3 dashes	hot sauce
1	can (14 oz.) creamed corn	2 cups	canned or thawed frozen corn kernels
1 tbsp.	sugar	1½ cups	shredded Cheddar cheese

1. Preheat oven to 375°F. Butter a 9- x 9- x 3-inch baking dish.

2. Whisk the eggs in a large bowl. Add the milk, cream, flour, creamed corn, sugar, baking powder, salt, pepper and hot sauce. Stir until combined. Fold in the corn kernels and Cheddar cheese. Pour into the baking dish.

3. Bake 45 to 50 minutes or until the top is golden brown and a knife inserted in the pudding comes out clean.

SERVES 8

Bourbon Baked Beans

A barbecue just isn't a barbecue without a crock full of baked beans. I like a little whisky in my recipe, but you can leave it out if you wish.

1 lb.	thick sliced bacon, cut in ½-inch pieces		¼ cup	malt vinegar
			2 tbsp.	mustard powder
3	onions, diced		2 tbsp.	Worcestershire sauce
8 cloves	garlic, minced		1 tbsp.	chopped fresh thyme
4	cans (each 14 oz.) baked beans (your favourite brand)		1 tsp.	black pepper
			1 tsp.	hot sauce
1 cup	ketchup			Salt
½ cup	molasses, honey or maple syrup		¼ cup	bourbon
½ cup	prepared mustard			

1. In a large saucepan fry the bacon until just crisp. Drain the bacon on paper towels. Drain all but 3 tbsp. of the bacon fat.

2. Add the onions and garlic; sauté for 4 to 5 minutes or until soft.

3. Add the baked beans, ketchup, molasses, prepared mustard, vinegar, mustard powder, Worcestershire sauce, thyme, pepper, hot sauce and crispy bacon.

4. Over medium-low heat, heat the beans for 20 to 30 minutes, stirring occasionally, until hot. Season to taste with salt, stir in the bourbon and serve.

SERVES 8 TO 10

Grilled Fingerling Potatoes and French Shallots

These crispy grilled potatoes make a great accompaniment to any steak or chicken dish.

1 lb.	fingerling potatoes		2 tbsp.	lemon juice
1 lb.	French shallots		1 tbsp.	chopped fresh rosemary
6 cloves	garlic, crushed		1 tsp.	cracked black pepper
¼ cup	olive oil			Lots of sea salt to taste

Tip

French shallots are long oval shallots. If you can't find them, use regular shallots. And if you can't find fingerlings, use mini white or red potatoes.

1. Boil the fingerling potatoes in a large pot of salted water for 10 to 12 minutes or until just tender. Drain, cool under cold water and pat dry.

2. Peel the shallots and cut in half lengthwise.

3. Preheat grill to medium-high.

4. In a large bowl toss together the potatoes, shallots, garlic, olive oil, lemon juice, rosemary, pepper and salt. Place mixture in a grill basket.

5. Grill for 10 to 12 minutes or until the potatoes are hot and slightly charred.

SERVES 6 TO 8

Cheddar Mashed Potatoes with Grilled Onions

I believe that mashed potatoes should be their own food group. Nothing is more comforting than a steaming bowl of mashed potatoes garnished with butter. If you should have leftovers of this recipe, make them into potato pancakes. Fry them in butter and serve with a poached egg.

2	large red onions, sliced ¼-inch thick		2 cups	shredded aged white Cheddar cheese
2 tbsp.	olive oil		½ cup	whipping cream
2 tbsp.	balsamic vinegar		¼ cup	finely chopped chives
1 tbsp.	Bone Dust BBQ Spice (page 97)		3 tbsp.	butter
2 lb.	Yukon Gold potatoes, peeled			Salt and pepper

1. Preheat grill to high.

2. In a large bowl carefully toss together the onions, olive oil, vinegar and BBQ spice. Place in a grill basket.

3. Grill for 10 to 12 minutes or until slightly charred and tender. Carefully remove onions from the basket and coarsely chop. Set aside.

4. In a large pot of salted water, boil the potatoes until tender, 15 to 20 minutes. Drain and return to the heat to dry the potatoes.

5. Remove from heat and mash the potatoes. Stir in the Cheddar cheese, cream, chives, butter and grilled onions. Season to taste with salt and pepper.

SERVES 6

Pamela's Potato and Cauliflower Hash

My lovely Pamela doesn't spend much time in the kitchen, but when she does get cooking it's always delicious. This is one of her recipes — and my favourite from her repertoire — that is perfect when served with eggs or steak.

⅓ head	cauliflower, broken into bite-sized pieces	2 cups	cubed cooked Yukon Gold potatoes
¼ cup	vegetable oil	1 tbsp.	chopped fresh parsley
3 cloves	garlic, minced	Pinch	cayenne pepper
1	large sweet onion, thinly sliced		Salt and freshly ground black pepper

1. Blanch the cauliflower for 2 to 3 minutes in boiling salted water. Drain and set aside.

2. Heat the oil in a large frying pan over medium-high heat. Sauté the garlic and onion, stirring constantly, for 12 to 15 minutes or until the onions are caramelized and slightly crisp. (This is the key to this recipe, as the sweet onions add a lot of flavour.) With a slotted spoon, transfer the mixture to a bowl.

3. Add a little more oil to your frying pan if necessary and fry the potatoes for 12 to 15 minutes, stirring occasionally, until crispy.

4. Add the onions and cauliflower to the pan and stir until mixed. Sauté for 4 to 5 minutes or until all is tender. Add the parsley and season to taste with a pinch of cayenne, salt and pepper. Stir thoroughly and serve immediately with fried eggs or grilled steak.

SERVES 4 TO 6

Love Potatoes (a.k.a. Super *!&#%*! Potatoes)

Note for the faint of heart: This is the potato dish of romance or heart attack, whichever comes first.

24	mini red or white potatoes		Salt and pepper to taste
2 tbsp.	olive oil	1 cup	shredded aged white Cheddar cheese
6 cloves	garlic, minced	1 cup	shredded mozzarella cheese
1	large onion, sliced	1 cup	shredded Monterey Jack cheese
¼ cup	chopped fresh herbs (such as sage, rosemary and thyme)	3 1½ to	eggs
2 tbsp.	balsamic vinegar	2 cups	whipping cream

1. Place the potatoes in a large pot and cover with cold water. Bring to a boil and season with a little salt. Reduce heat to medium and cook potatoes for 15 to 20 minutes or until tender. Drain and let cool.

2. Preheat oven to 375°F. Spray a 12- x 9-inch baking dish with nonstick cooking spray.

3. When the potatoes have cooled, press firmly on the top of each one to slightly smash and flatten it. Spread the potatoes in the greased baking dish.

4. In a frying pan over medium-high heat, heat the olive oil. Sauté the garlic and onion for 5 to 6 minutes, stirring occasionally, until lightly coloured and tender. Add the herbs, vinegar, salt and pepper.

5. Spread the onion mixture evenly over the potatoes. Combine the three cheeses and spread evenly over the onions.

6. In a bowl, whisk together the eggs and 1½ cups of the cream. Season to taste with salt and pepper. Pour over the potato/onion/cheese layers. Add additional cream if needed to just cover the layers.

7. Bake for 40 to 45 minutes or until the cheese is melted, golden brown and bubbling and the potatoes are hot. Let stand for 5 minutes.

8. Serve immediately with The Big Man's Coffee-Crusted Porterhouse steak (page 145), if desired.

SERVES 6

Baked Sweet Potatoes with Maple Orange Butter

Sweet potatoes are delicious when baked. The skin gets crisp and the flesh is tender. Drizzled with maple syrup or brown sugar, sweet potatoes make a great accompaniment to ribs and steaks.

8	sweet potatoes	8 tbsp.	Maple Orange Butter (recipe follows)
4	seedless oranges		Salt and pepper to taste

1. Preheat grill to high.

2. Cut each potato into ¼-inch slices about three-quarters of the way down but not all the way through. You should make at least 8 slices per sweet potato.

3. Thinly slice the oranges into rounds. You will need 32 slices (8 slices per orange). Cut each round in half.

4. Place 1 square of foil on top of another. Place 1 sweet potato on the foil. Insert 1 orange slice in each cut of the sweet potato. Crumble 1 tbsp. of the Maple Orange Butter on top of the sweet potato. Season with salt and pepper. Wrap foil tightly around the sweet potato.

5. Repeat with remaining sweet potatoes.

6. Grill sweet potatoes for 50 to 60 minutes or until they are tender when pierced with a knife.

7. Carefully unwrap the sweet potatoes and serve with extra Maple Orange Butter, if desired.

SERVES 8

Maple Orange Butter

This recipe makes more than you need for the baked sweet potatoes, but it's also great on French toast and pancakes. Freeze for up to 2 months.

½ lb.	unsalted butter, softened	1 tbsp.	chopped fresh thyme
¼ cup	chopped pecans	1 tsp.	orange zest
¼ cup	pure Canadian maple syrup	½ tsp.	coarsely ground black pepper
¼ cup	freshly squeezed orange juice		Salt to taste

1. In a food processor or mixing bowl, blend the butter, pecans, maple syrup, orange juice, thyme, orange zest, pepper and salt.

2. Place in a storage container and freeze until needed.

MAKES ABOUT 2 CUPS

Grilled Onion and Asparagus Risotto

Risotto can be flavoured with just about anything you wish. Grilled chicken, shrimp, lobster, corn and mushrooms make great additions to any risotto.

1	large red onion, sliced into rounds	4	shallots, finely chopped
1 lb.	asparagus	1 cup	Arborio rice
2 tbsp.	balsamic vinegar	¼ cup	medium-dry white wine
4 tbsp.	olive oil	4 cups	hot chicken stock
	Salt and freshly ground	1 tbsp.	chopped fresh thyme
	black pepper to taste	1 cup	shredded aged white Cheddar cheese

1. Preheat grill to medium-high.

2. In a large bowl toss together the onion, asparagus, balsamic vinegar, 2 tbsp. of the olive oil, salt and pepper. Place in a grill basket.

3. Grill onions and asparagus for 15 minutes, turning the basket periodically, until they are tender and lightly charred. Carefully remove onions and asparagus from the basket and cool slightly.

4. Coarsely chop the onions. Slice the asparagus spears into 1½-inch lengths. Set aside.

5. To prepare the risotto, in a large saucepan heat the remaining 2 tbsp. of oil over medium-high heat. Add the shallots; cook, stirring, for 30 seconds. Stir in the rice; cook for 1 minute, stirring constantly, or until the rice is evenly coated with oil.

6. Stir in the white wine and reduce liquid by half. Add ½ cup of the chicken stock, stirring constantly and waiting until most of the liquid is absorbed before adding more stock. Continue in this manner, adding ½ cup of stock at a time, until the rice is tender but slightly resistant to the bite, 15 to 20 minutes.

7. Stir in the onions, asparagus, thyme and Cheddar cheese. Season with salt and pepper.

8. Serve immediately with Apple Cider BBQ Atlantic Salmon (page 195), if desired.

SERVES 4

Finger Lickin'

Sandwiches

Pizza

The Ultimate Burger Garnish List

Ketchup

Mustard (prepared, Dijon, Pommery, honey mustard or spicy)

Relish (green, zucchini, tomato or corn)

Pickles (sour dills, bread and butter or kosher)

Onions (red, white, yellow, sweet or tart; raw, fried or grilled)

Salsa (mild, medium or hot) (page 41)

Guacamole (page 41)

Cheese (aged Cheddar, Swiss, Brie, Cambazola, mozzarella, blue cheese, jalapeño Jack or Muenster)

Back bacon

Bacon

Italian sausage patty

Bratwurst sausage

Fried egg

Grilled portobello mushrooms (page 58)

Lettuce (green leaf, red leaf, iceberg or romaine)

Tomato (red, yellow or green as long as they are fresh and full of flavour)

Peanut butter

Grilled vegetables (peppers, mushrooms, onions) (page 28)

Thousand Islands Dressing (page 18)

Green Goddess Ranch Dressing (page 15)

Sauerkraut

BBQ sauce

The Burger Is Better with Butter

I love a great hamburger. For years I searched in vain for the ultimate burger. But during that time, I did stumble across information on the original burger. These were fried — often in butter — and the buns were brushed with butter, then griddled. I decided to take this classic one step further: put the butter *in* the burger!

I made this burger once on my TV show *Cottage Country*. Piled with all the works, it must have been a foot high!

3 lb.	regular ground beef	1 tbsp.	Dijon mustard
4 tbsp.	butter, softened	Pinch	cayenne pepper
1	onion, finely chopped		Salt and freshly ground
3 cloves	garlic, minced		black pepper
1 tbsp.	chopped fresh parsley	6 or 12	burger buns
1 tbsp.	Worcestershire sauce	½ cup	melted butter (for brushing buns)

1. Preheat grill to medium-high.

2. In a large bowl, mix together the beef, butter, onion, garlic, parsley, Worcestershire sauce and Dijon mustard. Season to taste with cayenne pepper, salt and black pepper.

3. Form into twelve 4-oz. patties as uniform in size as possible. A flatter burger will cook more evenly and faster than a ball-like burger.

4. Grill burgers for 4 to 5 minutes per side for medium-well.

5. Brush burger buns with melted butter and grill cut side down until crisp and golden brown.

6. Serve with your favourite burger garnishes. I like the works, and my list of the works is obscene.

SERVES 6 OR 12

Aunt Corlis's Bread and Butter Pickles

My aunt Corlis makes the best pickles and relishes — awesome garnishes for burgers, hot dogs and sandwiches.

12	seedless cucumbers	1 tsp.	dill seed
6	onions, sliced	1 tsp.	mustard seeds
¼ cup	salt	1 tsp.	celery seeds
1½ cups	brown sugar	2 cups	cider vinegar
2 tsp.	turmeric		

1. Cut the cucumbers into ¼-inch slices. In a large bowl toss the cucumbers and onions with the salt. Cover with ice water and let soak for 4 hours.

2. Drain the cucumbers and onions and rinse with cold water. Let drain for 10 minutes.

3. In a large saucepan combine the sugar, turmeric, dill seed, mustard seeds, celery seeds and cider vinegar. Bring to a boil.

4. Add cucumbers and onions; heat for 5 minutes. Do not boil. Transfer to sterilized canning jars and seal at once.

MAKES ABOUT 4 QUARTS

Sweet Corn Relish

Sweet corn relish — made with fresh sweet peaches and cream corn — is one of my favourite garnishes for a hot dog or hamburger. To get the fresh kernels, hold a shucked ear upright in a bowl and with a sharp knife slice the kernels from the cob.

½ cup	corn flour	1	large green bell pepper, diced
¼ cup	mustard powder	4 cups	cider vinegar
1½ tbsp.	turmeric	2 cups	sugar
6 cups	peaches and cream corn kernels cut from the cob (about 12 ears)	2 tbsp.	salt
		1 tbsp.	mustard seeds
1½ cups	chopped green cabbage	1 tbsp.	celery seeds
4	red or sweet onions, diced	1 tbsp.	dried thyme
1	large red bell pepper, diced		

1. In a small bowl blend the corn flour, mustard powder and turmeric with a little cider vinegar to form a smooth paste.

2. In a large pot combine the turmeric paste, corn, cabbage, onions, bell peppers, vinegar, sugar, salt, mustard seeds, celery seeds and thyme. Bring to a boil. Reduce heat to medium-low and simmer, uncovered, for 45 minutes, stirring occasionally to prevent sticking.

3. Transfer to sterilized canning jars and seal at once.

MAKES ABOUT 4 QUARTS

Grilled Back Bacon on a Bun with Maple Beer BBQ Sauce

Also known as peameal bacon, back bacon is a salt-cured pork loin that is crusted with cornmeal. It can be purchased thinly sliced or in whole pieces. I prefer to buy a whole piece and slice it ½-inch thick. The presliced back bacon is too easy to overcook on the grill.

1½ lb.	whole back or peameal bacon (about 12 inches long)	**MAPLE BEER BBQ SAUCE**	
		1 bottle	beer
4	kaiser rolls, sliced	1 cup	BBQ sauce
4 slices	Cheddar cheese	½ cup	maple syrup
	Thinly sliced red onion	½ cup	grainy mustard
		3 cloves	garlic, minced
		2 tsp.	chopped fresh thyme
		1 tsp.	coarsely ground black pepper
		¼ tsp.	salt

1. Brush the bacon to remove the cornmeal crust. Slice the bacon into 24 slices, each ½-inch thick.

2. To prepare the sauce, in a saucepan bring the beer to a boil. Reduce heat and simmer until the beer has reduced by half. Add the BBQ sauce, maple syrup, mustard, garlic, thyme, pepper and salt. Return to a boil and simmer for 10 minutes, stirring occasionally. Remove from heat.

3. Meanwhile, preheat grill to medium-high.

4. Grill bacon for 2 to 3 minutes per side, basting liberally with beer BBQ sauce, until cooked through and tender.

5. Toast buns lightly. Places 6 slices of grilled bacon on the bottom half of each bun. Top with extra basting sauce, Cheddar cheese and onion slices, and finish with top half of bun.

MAKES 4 SANDWICHES

Tap House Grilled Cheese

This recipe is dedicated to the folks at the Tap House in Cleveland, Ohio — a bar that gives new meaning to the grilled cheese sandwich. This is my version of their great sandwich.

¼ cup	butter	16 slices	fried bacon
8 thick slices	Texas white bread	4 slices	Swiss cheese
8 thick slices	processed cheese	4 slices	beefsteak tomato
4 thin slices	red onion		Salt and pepper to taste
4 slices	Monterey Jack cheese		

1. Preheat grill to medium.

2. Butter one side of each slice of bread. Place 4 slices of bread butter side down.

3. Lay 1 slice of processed cheese in the centre of the bread. Top with the red onion, Jack cheese, bacon, Swiss cheese, tomato and another slice of processed cheese. Top with a slice of bread butter side up. Repeat for remaining sandwiches.

4. Grill sandwiches for 3 to 4 minutes per side, turning frequently to prevent burning, until the bread is golden brown and crisp and the cheese is melted.

5. Slice on the diagonal, season with salt and pepper and serve with ketchup.

MAKES 4 SANDWICHES

Grilled Honey Mustard Glazed Salmon Sandwich

While living in Banff, Alberta, I worked for Sunshine Ski Resort. During spring skiing season, a favourite lunchtime sandwich was grilled salmon on a crusty roll. My version of that sandwich incorporates sweet honey and honey mustard.

4	Atlantic salmon fillets (each 4 oz.), skinned	4 cloves	garlic, minced
			Salt and pepper
2 tbsp.	Salmon Seasoning (page 98)	8 slices	pumpernickel rye bread
2 tbsp.	vegetable oil	4 tbsp.	butter
¼ cup	grainy mustard	2 cups	Cucumber and Horseradish Salad (page 29)
¼ cup	honey	4 tbsp.	Green Goddess Ranch Dressing (page 15)
2 tbsp.	chopped fresh dill	4 leaves	green leaf lettuce
1 tbsp.	lemon juice		

1. Preheat grill to medium-high.

2. Season salmon fillets with Salmon Seasoning, rubbing the spice into the flesh. Brush salmon with oil.

3. Combine the mustard, honey, dill, lemon juice and garlic. Season to taste with salt and pepper.

4. Grill salmon for 3 to 4 minutes per side, basting with honey mustard glaze, until the salmon is medium doneness and lightly charred.

5. Grill rye bread until slightly crisp, and butter the slices. Top 4 slices of bread with the salmon. Top each with ½ cup of Cucumber and Horseradish Salad and drizzle with Green Goddess Ranch Dressing. Garnish with leaf lettuce and finish with a second slice of bread.

6. Serve immediately.

MAKES 4 SANDWICHES

My Cheese Steak Sandwich

Here's a melt-in-your-mouth sandwich for you. Using the tenderest cut of beef, it's loaded with sautéed onions and mushrooms and topped with Brie. Have lots of napkins on hand, for it's sure juicy.

4	beef tenderloin filets (each 6 oz.)	1 tbsp.	chopped fresh thyme
2 tbsp.	Great Canadian Steak Spice (page 97)	1 tbsp.	Dijon mustard
			Salt and pepper to taste
2 tbsp.	butter	8 slices	Brie
6 cloves	garlic, minced	4 slices	baguette (each about 4 inches long)
1	onion, diced	1 bunch	arugula
2 cups	sliced brown mushrooms		

1. Season beef with steak spice, rubbing the spice into the meat. Cover and set aside.

2. In a frying pan over medium-high heat, melt the butter. Sauté the garlic and onion for 2 to 3 minutes or until tender. Add the mushrooms; sauté for 10 to 15 minutes, stirring occasionally, until the liquid has evaporated and the mushrooms are tender. Remove from heat and add thyme, mustard, salt and pepper. Mix well. Set aside and keep warm.

3. Meanwhile, preheat grill to medium-high.

4. Grill steaks for 2 to 3 minutes per side for medium-rare.

5. Top each steak with a quarter of the mushroom mixture and 2 slices of Brie. Close the lid and grill until the cheese starts to melt.

6. Lightly toast each slice of baguette. Top with arugula and then the cheese steak.

MAKES 4 SANDWICHES

Chili Cheese Dogs

Some may say that the hot dog is what makes this sandwich, but I feel it's the bun and the condiments. Whether it's ketchup, mustard, relish, onion, sauerkraut, hot peppers or cheese, condiments are the key to making the dog taste good. I personally think that chili and cheese make the dog best. The messier it is, the better it is.

2 lb.	regular ground beef		2	cans (each 14 oz.) diced tomatoes
2 tsp.	ground cumin		3	poblano chili peppers, seeded and diced
2 tsp.	chili powder		2 tbsp.	chopped fresh cilantro
1 tsp.	black pepper		8	hot dogs
½ tsp.	salt		8	soft sesame egg hot dog rolls
1	large onion, diced		2 cups	shredded Cheddar cheese
4 cloves	garlic, minced			
2	cans (each 19 oz.) red kidney beans, rinsed and drained			

1. Season the beef with the cumin, chili powder, pepper and salt. In a frying pan over medium heat, brown the beef with the onions and garlic until the liquid has evaporated and the onions are brown, about 7 to 10 minutes. Stir in the red kidney beans, tomatoes and chilies. Simmer, uncovered, over medium heat for 1 hour, stirring occasionally to prevent scorching. Stir in the cilantro.

2. Preheat grill to medium-high.

3. Grill the hot dogs according to package instructions. Lightly toast the hot dog rolls. Place a hot dog in each roll. Pour a generous amount of chili over the hot dog. Top with Cheddar cheese.

4. Serve with plenty of napkins and, if desired, a side dish of extra chili.

SERVES 8

Grilled Turkey Steak Clubhouse with Praline Bacon

Next time you're in Waterloo, Ontario, have lunch at the Flying Dog Restaurant. The chef there pre-pares a praline-glazed bacon that is to die for. He uses a mix of brown sugar and ground walnuts. Since I'm not a walnut fan, I've substituted pecans.

4	boneless turkey steaks (each 5 oz.)	½ tsp.	vanilla
		½ tsp.	coarsely ground black pepper
2 tbsp.	Malabar Pepper Rub (page 96)	12 slices	thick bacon
¼ cup	cider vinegar	1	large beefsteak tomato
2 tbsp.	vegetable oil	8 slices	multi-grain bread
¼ cup	brown sugar		Mayonnaise
¼ cup	ground pecans	4 leaves	green leaf lettuce
2 tbsp.	water	1	small red onion, thinly sliced
1 tsp.	Worcestershire sauce	4 slices	Swiss cheese

1. Rub the turkey steaks with the pepper rub, pressing the seasoning into the flesh.

2. In a glass dish large enough to hold the turkey steaks, whisk together the vinegar and oil. Add the turkey steaks, turning to coat. Marinate, covered and refrigerated, for 2 hours.

3. In a small saucepan over medium heat, combine the brown sugar, pecans, water, Worcestershire sauce, vanilla and black pepper. Bring to a boil, reduce heat and simmer, stirring occasionally, for 5 minutes or until the syrup is thick. Set aside.

4. In a large frying pan, fry the bacon until it is just crisp. Add the brown sugar syrup. Turn the bacon to coat; remove from heat and keep warm.

5. Preheat grill to medium-high.

6. Grill turkey steaks for 4 to 5 minutes per side or until fully cooked and lightly charred.

7. Cut 8 thin slices from the tomato. Toast the bread slices. Spread 1 slice of toast with mayonnaise. Add lettuce, 2 tomato slices and red onion. Slice the turkey steak against the grain and lay over the onions. Add 3 slices of praline bacon, top with a slice of Swiss cheese and a second slice of toast. Repeat for remaining sandwiches.

MAKES 4 SANDWICHES

Grilled Lemon Chicken with Herbed Goat Cheese Spread and Roasted Red Peppers

This great summer picnic sandwich can be served hot or cold.

4	boneless skinless chicken breasts (each 6 oz.)	**HERBED GOAT CHEESE SPREAD**	
¼ cup	Herb Mustard Rub (page 100)	1	log (200 g) soft creamy goat cheese
¼ cup	lemon juice	¼ cup	lemon juice
2 tbsp.	olive oil	3	green onions, chopped
2	large red bell peppers, roasted, peeled, seeded and sliced	2 tbsp.	olive oil
		2 tbsp.	chopped fresh basil
		2 tbsp.	chopped fresh parsley
		1 tbsp.	chopped fresh mint
		1 tsp.	cracked black pepper
			Salt to taste
		1 loaf	sourdough black olive baguette
		1 bunch	arugula

1. Season the chicken with the Herb Mustard Rub. In a glass dish large enough to hold the chicken, whisk together the lemon juice and olive oil. Add the chicken, turning to coat. Marinate, covered and refrigerated, for 4 hours.

2. Meanwhile, prepare the Herbed Goat Cheese Spread by combining the goat cheese, lemon juice, green onions, olive oil, basil, parsley, mint, pepper and salt. Cover and refrigerate until needed.

3. Preheat grill to medium-high.

4. Slice the baguette diagonally into eight 1-inch-thick slices. Brush one side of each slice with olive oil.

5. Grill the chicken breasts for 5 to 6 minutes per side or until fully cooked and golden brown. Remove from grill and thinly slice against the grain.

Continued . . .

6. Lightly grill the bread slices olive oil side down.

7. Place arugula leaves on 4 slices of bread. Top each with a chicken breast. Top with roasted red peppers. Spread the goat cheese on the remaining 4 slices of bread and top sandwiches.

8. Serve immediately.

SERVES 4

Grilled Muffuletta Sandwich

This recipe is offered in celebration of the 40 or 50 muffuletta sandwiches that I have eaten at Central Grocery in New Orleans. Serve this grilled version with an ice-cold beer.

3	boneless skinless chicken breasts (each 6 oz.)	**OLIVE SALAD**	
1½ tbsp.	Bone Dust BBQ Spice (page 97)	1½ cups	sliced pimento-stuffed green olives
		1	small red onion, diced
3 cloves	garlic, minced	1 stalk	celery, finely diced
2 tbsp.	olive oil	1	green bell pepper, diced
2 tbsp.	red wine vinegar	1	red bell pepper, diced
8 slices	pancetta	4	green onions, chopped
1 loaf	round Italian bread	3 cloves	garlic, minced
6 leaves	green leaf lettuce	¼ cup	grated Parmesan cheese
2	tomatoes, thinly sliced	¼ cup	olive oil
½	small seedless cucumber, thinly sliced diagonally	2 tbsp.	red wine vinegar
		1 tbsp.	chopped flat-leaf parsley
		1 tbsp.	chopped fresh basil
8 slices	prosciutto	1 tbsp.	Dijon mustard
8 slices	spicy capocollo	1 tsp.	crushed chilies
8 slices	provolone cheese		Salt and pepper to taste

1. Rub the chicken breasts with the BBQ spice. In a glass dish large enough to hold the chicken, whisk together the garlic, olive oil and vinegar. Add chicken, turning to coat. Cover and refrigerate for 4 to 6 hours.

2. To make the salad, in a bowl combine the olives, onion, celery, green and red peppers, green onions, garlic, Parmesan cheese, olive oil, vinegar, parsley, basil, mustard, crushed chilies, salt and pepper. Mix well, cover and refrigerate. (Salad can be made a few hours in advance.)

3. Preheat grill to medium-high.

4. Grill chicken for 5 to 6 minutes per side or until cooked through. Let cool. Grill pancetta for 1 to 2 minutes per side or until crisp. Drain on paper towels. Thinly slice cooled chicken.

Continued . . .

5. Slice the top off the loaf of bread. (Don't eat the top — you will need it for the lid.) Scoop out the middle to make a bread bowl, leaving a wall about ½-inch thick. Spoon in half of the olive salad. Top with lettuce, tomatoes and cucumbers. Add the chicken, pancetta, prosciutto, capocollo and provolone cheese. Top with remaining olive salad. Cover with the bread lid, wrap tightly in plastic wrap and refrigerate for 1 hour.

6. Cut loaf into 6 or 8 wedges and serve with a green salad and ice-cold beer. (Try a Dixie — that's what I drink with my Central Grocery muffuletta.)

SERVES 1, 2, 3 OR 4

Seaside Grilled Shrimp Fajitas with Mango Salsa

There is a little restaurant in Seaside, California, called Turtle Bay. Over the past few years I have had the pleasure of eating a few meals there. It is just what a chef needs after a full day of cooking on the race circuit at Laguna Seca. This is my version of this tasty dish.

16	jumbo shrimp, peeled and deveined	4	flour tortillas (10 inch)
		1 cup	Black Bean Paste (recipe follows)
2 tbsp.	Herb Mustard Rub (page 100)	1 cup	Mango Salsa (recipe follows)
2 tbsp.	olive oil	2 cups	Firecracker Coleslaw (page 35)

1. Soak 4 bamboo skewers in hot water for 30 minutes. (Or use metal skewers.)

2. In a bowl combine the shrimp, Herb Mustard Rub and olive oil. Toss to evenly coat shrimp. Thread 4 shrimp onto each skewer. Marinate, covered and refrigerated, for 20 minutes.

3. Preheat grill to high.

4. Grill shrimp for 2 to 3 minutes per side or until opaque in colour and the shrimp are tender and just done. Keep warm on grill.

5. Warm the tortillas on the hot grill for 30 seconds per side.

6. Spread 1 tortilla with ¼ cup black bean paste. Top with 1 skewer of shrimp, removing the skewer. Top with 1 or 2 tbsp. mango salsa and finish with ½ cup coleslaw.

7. Fold the bottom quarter of the tortilla up to the centre. Starting from the side, roll the tortilla into a cylinder. Repeat with remaining tortillas.

8. Serve with extra salsa, guacamole (page 40) and sour cream.

SERVES 4

Tip

Use the leftover black bean paste and mango salsa as a dip for potato chips or tortilla chips.

Continued …

Black Bean Paste

1½ cups	cooked black beans, rinsed and drained if canned	2	jalapeño peppers, chopped
		3	green onions, chopped
1 tbsp.	lemon juice	1 clove	garlic, minced
1 tsp.	Bone Dust BBQ Spice (page 97)	½ cup	frozen sweet corn kernels, thawed
1 tbsp.	chopped fresh cilantro		Salt and pepper to taste

1. In a food processor blend until smooth the black beans, lemon juice and BBQ spice.

2. Add the cilantro, jalapeño peppers, green onions and garlic. Pulse to blend.

3. Transfer bean mixture to a mixing bowl. Add the corn, salt and pepper. Mix thoroughly. Refrigerate at least 1 hour before using.

MAKES 2 CUPS

Mango Salsa

1	ripe mango, peeled, seeded and diced	1	lime, juiced
		1 tbsp.	chopped fresh cilantro
1	small red onion, diced	1 tbsp.	olive oil
2	green onions, chopped	Dash	hot sauce
1 clove	garlic, minced		Salt and pepper

1. In a bowl combine the mango, red onion, green onions, garlic, lime juice, cilantro and olive oil. Season to taste with hot sauce, salt and pepper.

MAKES ABOUT 2 CUPS

Quick BBQ Pizza Dough

This simple recipe for pizza dough requires no proofing time. Perfect for when you're in a hurry.

1 cup	all-purpose flour	¼ cup	butter, diced
1 cup	corn flour	½ to	
¼ cup	grated Parmesan cheese	⅔ cup	milk
1 tbsp.	Bone Dust BBQ Spice (page 97)		
1 tbsp.	chopped fresh cilantro	**Special equipment: 1 perforated pizza pan**	
2½ tsp.	baking powder		

1. In a bowl stir together the all-purpose flour, corn flour, 2 tbsp. of the Parmesan cheese, BBQ spice, cilantro and baking powder. Add butter; rub in with fingertips until the mixture resembles coarse bread crumbs.

2. Stir in enough milk to form a dough. Turn out onto a lightly floured surface and knead for 2 to 3 minutes or until dough is smooth. (If not using dough immediately, wrap in plastic wrap and refrigerate until needed.)

3. Roll out the dough to a 10-inch circle. Transfer to a perforated pizza pan.

To parbake the pizza crust

1. Preheat oven to 425°F.

2. Brush pizza dough with olive oil. Sprinkle with remaining 2 tbsp. Parmesan cheese, salt and pepper.

3. Bake for 6 to 8 minutes or until the dough is partially cooked and lightly coloured.

4. Use immediately in the following recipes or with your favourite sauce and toppings.

MAKES DOUGH FOR ONE 10-INCH PIZZA

BBQ Chicken Pizza with Artichokes and Four Cheeses

Pizza is the most popular finger food after potato chips and French fries. A summer barbecue wouldn't be complete without a great pizza.

For the chicken, try my Devil's Brewed Roast Chicken (page 184).

¼ to		1 cup	shredded Monterey Jack cheese
½ cup	BBQ sauce	1	jar (6 oz.) marinated artichoke hearts, drained
1	Quick BBQ Pizza Dough	2 cups	shredded grilled chicken
	(page 91), parbaked	1	small red onion, sliced
1 cup	shredded Swiss cheese	½ cup	crumbled goat cheese
1 cup	shredded mozzarella cheese	1 tbsp.	chopped fresh cilantro

1. Preheat grill to medium.

2. Spread the BBQ sauce evenly over the pizza crust, leaving a ½-inch border around the edge.

3. Combine the Swiss, mozzarella and Monterey Jack cheeses. Sprinkle evenly over the pizza.

4. Quarter the artichoke hearts and pat dry with paper towels. Arrange the artichoke hearts, chicken and red onion on top of the cheese. Sprinkle with goat cheese. Transfer to a perforated pizza pan.

5. Grill the pizza, with the lid closed, for 5 to 7 minutes or until the cheese melts and the toppings are hot. Check periodically to see that the crust is not burning. If the crust darkens too quickly, reduce heat to low and continue to grill.

6. Remove pizza from grill, sprinkle with cilantro and cut into 6 slices.

SERVES 2 TO 3

Shrimp and Brie Pizza with Almond Pesto

The beauty of pizza is that you can put anything you want on top. Here, the richness of the Brie blends well with shrimp. If you are not a fan of shrimp, try crab, lobster or even smoked salmon. A delicious twist on a classic.

⅓ cup	Almond Pesto (recipe follows)	1 tbsp.	olive oil
1	Quick BBQ Pizza Dough (page 91), parbaked	1	small wheel Brie (125 g)
1 lb.	jumbo shrimp, peeled and deveined	1	small sweet onion (Vidalia, Texas Sweet or Maui), sliced
1 tbsp.	Bay Seasoning (page 98)	¼ cup	grated Parmesan cheese

1. Preheat grill to medium.

2. Spread the almond pesto evenly over the pizza crust, leaving a ½-inch border at the edge.

3. Pat the shrimp dry with paper towels. Slice each shrimp in half lengthwise. In a bowl toss the shrimp with Bay Seasoning and olive oil. Lay the shrimp evenly over the sauce.

4. Using a sharp knife, cut white rind from the Brie. Cut the Brie into ¼-inch-thick slices and then into 1-inch squares. Lay Brie on top of shrimp. Sprinkle with onion slices and Parmesan cheese. Transfer to a perforated pizza pan.

5. Grill the pizza, with the lid closed, for 5 to 7 minutes or until the cheese melts and the toppings are hot. Check periodically that the crust is not burning. If the crust darkens too quickly, reduce heat to low and continue to grill.

6. Remove pizza from grill and cut into 6 slices.

SERVES 2 TO 3

Continued ...

Almond Pesto

1	large bunch fresh basil	2 tbsp.	hot water
½ cup	chopped flat-leaf parsley	1 tbsp.	lemon juice
½ cup	toasted slivered almonds	1 tsp.	black pepper
¼ cup	grated Parmesan cheese	½ tsp.	salt
6 cloves	garlic, chopped	⅔ cup	olive oil
2 tbsp.	chopped fresh dill		

1. Wash the basil and remove the leaves; pat dry. In a food processor combine the basil, parsley, almonds, Parmesan cheese, garlic, dill, water, lemon juice, pepper and salt. Blend until finely chopped. With the motor running, add the oil in a steady stream until fully incorporated. If the mixture is too thick add a little more hot water to give you a better spreading consistency.

MAKES 1½ CUPS

Rubbin' Is Lovin'

Seasoning Rubs and Pastes

Malabar Pepper Rub

The Malabar coast of India is best known for its black pepper. This rub is a variation of one I discovered on an expedition to Cochin, India.

This is a great rub for beef, chicken and salmon.

¼ cup	cracked black peppercorns
¼ cup	crushed red chilies
¼ cup	coarse kosher salt
2 tbsp.	granulated garlic
2 tbsp.	granulated onion
1 tbsp.	sugar
1 tbsp.	curry powder
1 tbsp.	ground coriander

1. In a bowl mix together the black pepper, crushed red chilies, salt, garlic, onion, sugar, curry and coriander.

2. Store in an airtight container in a cool, dry place away from heat and light.

MAKES ABOUT 1¼ CUPS

Gilroy Roasted Garlic Paste

Not all rubs are dry rubs. This paste recipe uses lots of freshly roasted garlic. I remember driving through the town of Gilroy, California. The smell of fresh garlic filled the car—with the windows up!

Rub this paste liberally into chicken, lamb or beef cuts.

3	large heads garlic
½ cup	(approx.) olive oil
¼ cup	grainy mustard
2 tbsp.	chopped fresh parsley
2 tbsp.	chopped fresh rosemary
2 tbsp.	coarsely ground black pepper
1 tbsp.	coarse kosher salt
1 tbsp.	balsamic vinegar

1. Preheat oven to 325°F.

2. Separate the cloves of garlic and peel them. Place in an ovenproof dish just large enough to hold them. Add enough olive oil to cover the garlic. Roast garlic for 30 to 45 minutes or until golden brown and tender. Let cool.

3. In a food processor place the roasted garlic and ½ cup of the garlic-roasted olive oil. Add the mustard, parsley, rosemary, pepper, salt and vinegar. Blend until smooth.

4. Store, refrigerated, for up to 2 weeks.

MAKES ABOUT 2 CUPS

Great Canadian Steak Spice (a.k.a. Montreal Steak Spice)

This has got to be the best rub for steaks. I believe that the saltier the rub, the better the steak will be.

½ cup	coarse kosher salt
¼ cup	coarsely ground black pepper
¼ cup	coarsely ground white pepper
¼ cup	mustard seeds
¼ cup	cracked coriander seeds
¼ cup	granulated garlic
¼ cup	granulated onion
¼ cup	crushed red chilies
¼ cup	dill seed

1. Combine the salt, black pepper, white pepper, mustard seeds, coriander seeds, garlic, onion, crushed chilies and dill seed.

2. Store in an airtight container in a cool, dry place away from heat and light.

MAKES 2½ CUPS

Bone Dust BBQ Spice (a.k.a. The Best BBQ Rub)

As you may well know, I love to grill. Well, this is my favourite recipe for a BBQ spice. It is from my *Sticks and Stones Cookbook*. It just doesn't get any better than this one.

½ cup	paprika
¼ cup	chili powder
3 tbsp.	salt
2 tbsp.	ground coriander
2 tbsp.	garlic powder
2 tbsp.	sugar
2 tbsp.	curry powder
2 tbsp.	hot mustard powder
1 tbsp.	black pepper
1 tbsp.	dried basil
1 tbsp.	dried thyme
1 tbsp.	ground cumin
1 tbsp.	cayenne pepper

1. Mix together the paprika, chili powder, salt, coriander, garlic powder, sugar, curry powder, mustard powder, black pepper, basil, thyme, cumin and cayenne.

2. Store in an airtight container in a cool, dry place away from heat and light.

MAKES ABOUT 2½ CUPS

Salmon Seasoning

I love salmon. I think growing up with a Newfie dad had something to do with this. Here's a tasty seasoning that blends nicely with the richness of salmon.

¼ cup	lemon pepper
¼ cup	coarse kosher salt
¼ cup	dill seed
¼ cup	ground coriander
2 tbsp.	dried dill
1 tbsp.	paprika
1 tbsp.	granulated garlic
1 tbsp.	granulated onion
2 tsp.	cayenne pepper
2 tsp.	sugar

1. Combine the lemon pepper, salt, dill seed, coriander, dill, paprika, garlic, onion, cayenne and sugar.

2. Store in an airtight container in a cool, dry place away from heat and light.

MAKES ABOUT 1½ CUPS

Bay Seasoning

Inspired by the countless days I spent crabbing on Chesapeake Bay, here is a classic seasoning for crab boils, shrimp boils and clam bakes. The most famous of its kind is Old Bay Seasoning, a truly excellent seasoning. I think mine is just a little better, of course, but if you don't have the time to prepare this recipe by all means use Old Bay.

½ cup	paprika
¼ cup	celery salt
¼ cup	coarse kosher salt
¼ cup	cayenne pepper
¼ cup	ground black pepper
¼ cup	ground white pepper
¼ cup	garlic powder
¼ cup	onion powder
¼ cup	ground coriander
¼ cup	ground cumin
2 tbsp.	sugar
1 tbsp.	curry powder

1. Combine the paprika, celery salt, salt, cayenne, black pepper, white pepper, garlic powder, onion powder, coriander, cumin, sugar and curry powder.

2. Store in an airtight container in a cool, dry place away from heat and light.

MAKES ABOUT 3 CUPS

Hell's Fire Chili Paste

Some folks just like it to be insanely hot. So here it is. Blow your brains out with this rubbing paste. Good luck, and remember to keep lots of water on hand. Also, you may want to use rubber gloves and a mask when preparing this.

1	can (7 oz.) smoked chipotle chilies
6	habanero chili peppers
3	green onions, coarsely chopped
4 cloves	garlic
2	limes, juiced
¼ cup	chopped fresh cilantro
¼ cup	olive oil
1 tbsp.	sugar
2 tsp.	salt

1. In a food processor combine the chipotle chilies, habanero chili peppers, green onions, garlic, lime juice, cilantro, olive oil, sugar and salt. Blend until smooth.

2. Transfer to a small dish. Cover and refrigerate. Keeps for up to 2 weeks.

MAKES ABOUT 1½ CUPS

Mocha Coffee Rub

I love the flavour of coffee, and it has a wonderful affinity with beef and lamb.

I don't recommend using a coffee grinder here because the coffee needs to be coarse, not finely ground.

½ cup	mocha-flavoured coffee beans
6 cloves	garlic, minced
¼ cup	chopped fresh rosemary
¼ cup	chopped fresh parsley
¼ cup	cracked black pepper
¼ cup	olive oil
2 tbsp.	molasses
2 tbsp.	balsamic vinegar
	Salt to taste

1. Using the bottom of a heavy frying pan, crush the coffee beans.

2. Stir together the crushed coffee beans, garlic, rosemary, parsley, black pepper, olive oil, molasses, balsamic vinegar and salt.

3. Store, refrigerated, in a sealed container. Keeps up to 2 weeks.

MAKES ABOUT 2 CUPS

Herb Mustard Rub

I love to use fresh herbs whenever possible. This combination of fresh herbs and mustard is a great way to enhance poultry and pork.

1 cup	chopped fresh herbs (any combination of parsley, sage, rosemary, thyme, tarragon, dill and savory)
6 cloves	garlic, minced
¼ cup	Dijon mustard
¼ cup	grainy mustard
2 tbsp.	honey
2 tbsp.	white wine vinegar
¼ cup	olive oil
1 tbsp.	coarsely ground black pepper
	Salt to taste

1. Combine the herbs, garlic, Dijon mustard, grainy mustard, honey, vinegar, oil, black pepper and salt.

2. Store, refrigerated, in a sealed container. Keeps up to 2 weeks.

MAKES ABOUT 2 CUPS

Indonesian Cinnamon Rub

Cinnamon adds a natural sweetness to certain foods. It is not just for baking but is an excellent addition to many savoury dishes.

This rub can be used on chicken, lamb and pork dishes.

¼ cup	cinnamon
2 tbsp.	sugar
2 tbsp.	ground cumin
2 tbsp.	ground allspice
1 tbsp.	ground cloves
1 tbsp.	ground ginger
1 tbsp.	garlic powder
1 tbsp.	salt

1. Combine cinnamon, sugar, cumin, allspice, cloves, ginger, garlic powder and salt.

2. Store in an airtight container in a cool, dry place away from heat and light.

MAKES ABOUT 1 CUP

Jamaican Jerk Paste

This great recipe has been handed down to my dear friend Bridget from her family in Jamaica. It brings out the zing in any dish. The name "jerk" can only be attributed to the sudden rush your palate feels when eating it.

4	habanero or	¼ cup	olive oil
	Scotch bonnet peppers	¼ cup	lemon juice
6	green onions, coarsely chopped	2 tbsp.	ground allspice
¼ cup	water	2 tsp.	salt
1 cup	fresh cilantro leaves	1 tsp.	ground cloves
1 cup	fresh parsley leaves	1 tsp.	ground cumin
6 cloves	garlic	1 tsp.	black pepper

1. In a food processor or blender, purée the habanero peppers, green onions and water. Add the cilantro, parsley and garlic; purée until smooth. Add the olive oil, lemon juice, allspice, salt, cloves, cumin and black pepper. Blend until fully incorporated.

2. Store in a sealed container, refrigerated. Keeps up to 2 weeks.

MAKES ABOUT 3 CUPS

Tip

Jerk is a great seasoning for pork and chicken.

Miami Spice Love Paste

Try this sweet and spicy rub on fish, shellfish, chicken or ribs.

2 tbsp.	orange zest	2	red finger chili peppers
½ cup	orange juice	4	green onions, coarsely chopped
½ cup	fresh cilantro leaves	2 tsp.	salt
¼ cup	chopped fresh ginger	2 tsp.	ground fennel
¼ cup	olive oil	1 tsp.	cinnamon
¼ cup	Grand Marnier	1 tsp.	black pepper
6 cloves	garlic		

1. In a food processor or blender, combine the orange zest and juice, cilantro, ginger, olive oil, Grand Marnier, garlic, chili peppers, green onions, salt, fennel, cinnamon and pepper. Blend until smooth.

2. Store, refrigerated, in a sealed container. Keeps up to 2 weeks.

MAKES ABOUT 2 CUPS

Licorice Rub

Toasting the spices extracts their natural oils, which will bring out more flavour in your recipes. Use this rub on chicken and lamb.

½ cup	fennel seeds
¼ cup	black peppercorns
4	star anise, broken into pieces
3	3-inch cinnamon sticks, broken into small pieces
1 tsp.	whole cloves
1 tbsp.	granulated garlic
1 tbsp.	ground ginger
1 tbsp.	salt

1. Heat a frying pan over medium heat. Toast the fennel, peppercorns, star anise, cinnamon sticks and whole cloves for 3 to 5 minutes or until lightly toasted and fragrant.

2. Using a spice/coffee mill, grind the spices into a fine powder. In a bowl, stir together the ground spices, garlic, ginger and salt.

3. Store in an airtight container in a cool, dry place away from heat and light.

MAKES ABOUT ¾ CUP

Red-Rum Rub

This is a fiery paste ("red rum" spelled backwards is …) that will make you blush.

8	red finger chili peppers
1	small red onion, peeled and quartered
1	red bell pepper, seeded and quartered
½ cup	red chili oil
8 cloves	garlic
¼ cup	red paprika
¼ cup	amber rum
2 tsp.	red cayenne pepper
1 tsp.	salt

1. Preheat oven to 375°F.

2. In an ovenproof dish toss together the red finger chili peppers, red onion, red bell pepper, red chili oil and garlic. Roast for 30 to 45 minutes or until all is very lightly charred and tender.

3. In a food processor or blender, purée the mixture until smooth. Add the red paprika, rum, red cayenne pepper and salt. Mix until incorporated.

4. Store, refrigerated, in a sealed container. Keeps up to 2 weeks.

MAKES ABOUT 2 CUPS

Rib Stickin'

Rib Basics

Pork Ribs

Beef Ribs

Lamb Ribs

Rib Types

Pork Baby Back Ribs

Baby back ribs are the ultimate rib. Cut from the loin, they are much leaner than spareribs and tend to have a higher meat-to-bone ratio. When prepared properly, these ribs provide the best eating. I recall once organizing the SkyDome Ribfest, a promotion for Loblaws Grocery Stores, during which we cooked a million pounds of baby back ribs.

Whether the ribs are fresh or frozen, look for ribs that have more loin meat attached. A baby back rib should weigh between 1¼ and 2 lb. Baby back ribs are more expensive than spareribs but are the best quality. As the saying goes, "You get what you pay for."

Pork Spareribs

Spareribs are cut from the side, or underbelly, of the pig. These ribs are quite meaty but are also fattier than baby back ribs. Weighing usually between 2½ and 3½ lb., these ribs can serve several people. Spareribs are usually sold with the soft bone brisket attached. This cartilage material is tough and fatty and is best trimmed off and used in soup stocks. Ask your butcher to remove the brisket for you.

The term "St. Louis rib" means that the soft bone brisket has been removed, which produces a rib that is more uniform in size and makes for easier cooking and eating. These ribs usually weigh around 2 lb.

Country-Style Pork Ribs

Country-style pork ribs are extremely meaty. In fact, there are usually just a few small bones attached. These ribs come from the rib end of the pork loin and are loaded with meat. They're priced less than baby back ribs and spareribs. These ribs require a little longer cooking time to ensure tenderness but are well worth the wait.

Pork Back Rib Tail Pieces

I was involved in developing a product for President's Choice® called If Pigs Could Fly. This was a frozen appetizer that used a byproduct of the pork baby back rib. When the butcher prepares pork baby back ribs, the small "tail" piece must be removed from the end of the rib. Tail pieces are approximately 6 to 8 inches long and have small flat bones. They are to pork what the wing is to chicken — a great snack food.

Rib tail pieces are not always available and are best ordered through your favourite butcher. Allow at least 4 to 6 pieces per person.

Pork Shoulder

A whole pork shoulder consists of the blade bone, shank and foreleg and weighs approximately 15 to 20 lb. This is a lot of meat, and unless you are feeding a crowd of people and have a lot of time on your hands I do not recommend purchasing a whole shoulder. The whole shoulder is used in BBQ competitions.

You can find at your local butcher or grocery store smaller cuts from the shoulder area. The picnic roast, or shoulder roast (a.k.a. Boston butt), is a smaller cut (approximately 5 to 7 lb.) and easier to prepare. The best method for preparation is to slowly smoke the shoulder pieces over low heat. Low and slow makes for succulent and tender.

Beef Ribs

These are enormous ribs that are cut from the loin of beef. They are best ordered from your favourite butcher, since most grocery stores do not carry them. They're usually bought up by the food service industry, which does not leave too many ribs for the retailer. As a chef at the SkyDome, I prepared many prime ribs of beef for our customers. I would often remove the back ribs after the beef was cooked and then grill the ribs and baste them generously with a smoky BBQ sauce. These ribs never made it to the customer, as I would serve them to my staff as a dinner treat.

"Monster Bones" or "Dinosaur Ribs," as they are frequently referred to on menus, are succulent and meaty. Have a lot of napkins on hand because the only true way to eat these is with your hands.

Beef Short Ribs

This inexpensive cut of meat is readily available in grocery stores. It is cut from the belly plate, or the chuck areas, of a steer and is composed of layers of meat, fat and flat rib bones. The fat cap of a short rib should be trimmed before cooking. These ribs are quite chunky and take a fair amount of time to cook.

You may also purchase what are called Maui or Miami ribs, depending where you are from. These ribs are cut approximately ½-inch thick across the short ribs. They have 4 or 5 bones in each and can be prepared quickly on the grill once they are marinated.

Lamb Ribs

Lamb ribs are popular in South Africa, Australia and in the South Pacific but are not as well known to North American barbecue aficionados. Lamb ribs are smaller than pork ribs, weighing in at just around a pound. Lamb ribs have a thick fat cap, which should be removed before cooking. There is not a lot of meat on lamb ribs, so allow 2 racks per person. If you are a lover of lamb, then these ribs will make you really smile.

Cooking Methods

Boiling

Some chefs say never to boil ribs. I believe that you can — but make sure that you add some kind of flavouring to the water. Boiling ribs tends to remove the flavour and succulence from the meat, so you need to add something to replace the lost flavour, such as apple cider, pineapple juice, beer, ginger ale or stock. Boiling is not my most favourite method of cooking ribs, but it does tenderize them. I would recommend boiling only pork spareribs and never boiling beef or lamb ribs.

Cooking Time: Cooking liquid temperature 210°F.
Allow approximately 30 minutes
    per lb.
2 to 3 lb. spareribs   90 minutes
1 to 2 lb. back ribs   60 minutes

Steaming

My friend Dave Nichol swears by steaming for cooking tender pork ribs. I agree with him. Steaming ribs allows the meat to tenderize without losing its flavour to the water, as in boiling. A large steamer pot will do the job. Flavour the steaming liquid with garlic, onions and assorted herbs and spices before steaming the ribs. Never steam beef ribs.

Cooking Time: Bring cooking liquid to a boil.
Place steamer insert in pot and
    add ribs.
Allow approximately 30 minutes
    per lb.
2 to 3 lb. spareribs   90 minutes
1 to 2 lb. back ribs   60 minutes
1 lb. lamb ribs   45 minutes

Oven Roasting

Oven roasting is a great way to cook ribs. This method suits all types of ribs (pork, beef and lamb). When preparing ribs for roasting, always rub them with a BBQ seasoning of some flavour. (See the "Rubbin' Is Lovin'" chapter for rubs.) Preheat your oven to 350°F and place seasoned ribs on a wire rack in a roasting pan.

Cooking Time: Preheated 350°F oven.
2 to 3 lb. spareribs
    and beef ribs   75 to 90 minutes
1 to 2 lb. back rib and
    country-style ribs   60 to 75 minutes
1 lb. lamb ribs   45 to 60 minutes

Grilling

In this method of cooking, ribs are cooked fully on the grill, whereas boiling, steaming, roasting, smoking and braising all require that you finish the ribs on a hot grill before serving.

Grilling ribs requires low heat, patience and desire. These three "principles" will produce a great-tasting rib. Grilling is best suited for pork back and spareribs.

The temperature of your grill should remain at around 325°F. Since cooking on a grill is with dry heat, you need to have some moisture to keep the ribs from drying out. Place a small pan of water in the bottom of the grill among the coals or on top of the grill bars. Marinate your ribs for 4 to 6 hours and then rub them with your favourite BBQ seasoning. Place them on the grill meaty side up, close the lid and cook the ribs until the meat is tender. Near the end of the cooking brush the ribs with your favourite BBQ sauce.

Cooking Time: Preheated 325°F grill.
2 to 3 lb. spareribs
and beef ribs   90 minutes
1 to 2 lb. pork
back ribs and
country-style ribs 75 minutes
1 lb. lamb ribs   60 minutes

Smoking

Smoking ribs — or real barbecue — is as much an art form as it is a method of cooking. Various styles of smokers are available for backyard use. Whatever kind you use, three basic principles apply. They're the same three principles of grilling ribs but with a few changes. Low heat is a must — around 200 to 225°F. You must have more patience (smoking can take anywhere from 3 to 7 hours, depending on the size and cut of your meat), and your desire will grow. So sit back, relax, crack a cold one and tend to your ribs.

For best results, use a charcoal smoker. You can smoke on a gas grill, but true lovers of barbecue smoke only over coals with flavoured wood chips. Heat a small amount of charcoal to between 200 and 225°F.

Soak smoking chips in water for at least 1 hour before adding to hot coals. You will need to replenish these chips every so often during the smoking. Try a variety of flavoured smoking chips. Hickory and mesquite are the most popular, but cherry, apple and maple chips offer great flavour as well. When in the South I like to use pecan wood. It provides a sweet nutty flavour to my smoked ribs.

When the coals are hot, place a dish of hot water in the bottom of the smoker. Place the grill on top of the hot coals.

It is best to marinate your ribs for 4 to 6 hours or overnight and then rub them with your favourite spice rub. Place ribs meaty side up and cover the smoker. Once an hour, check and add additional coals and smoking chips as needed, maintaining the temperature around 200 to 225°F.

Cooking Time: Preheated 200 to 225°F smoker.
Soaked smoking chips.
2 to 3 lb. pork spareribs
and beef ribs   3 to 4 hours
6 to 8 lb. pork picnic or
pork butt roasts   5 to 6 hours
1 to 2 lb. pork
back ribs and
country-style ribs   3 hours

Braising: My Favourite Cooking Method

I love cooking ribs as much as I love eating ribs. I started out like many, boiling and steaming ribs, but was never satisfied with the results. I then started travelling to different BBQ competitions in search of the best ribs. I learned to love smoked ribs and grilled ribs but knew that the ultimate rib had to be somewhere out there. I then met a rib cooker by the name of Jerry Gibson. Jerry's ribs were incredible. Nirvana was at hand. Jerry told me that braising was the secret to great-tasting ribs. Braising is done in your oven and is a combination of roasting and steaming.

Preheat oven to 325°F. Rub ribs with your favourite BBQ seasoning. Place ribs meat side down overlapping in a roasting pan. Add 1 to 2 cups of liquid (juice, beer or water) and place 3 to 4 slices of lemon on the back of each rack of ribs. Cover and braise until fully cooked and the bones can be pulled cleanly from the meat.

Cooking Time: Preheated 325°F oven.

2 to 3 lb. pork spareribs and beef ribs, beef short ribs	2 to 3 hours
1 to 2 lb. pork back ribs and country-style ribs	2 to 2½ hours
1 lb. lamb ribs	1½ hours

South Carolina Yellow Back Ribs

Yellow BBQ sauce is a South Carolina favourite and is made from prepared mustard. It's tangy, sweet and a little spicy, with a golden colour that delights the eye. Don't use any of those fancy mustards for this recipe. Basic bright yellow prepared mustard is what makes this recipe sing.

4 racks	baby back ribs (each 1½ lb.)	1 cup	prepared mustard
2 tbsp.	Bone Dust BBQ Spice (page 97)	¾ cup	cider vinegar
2	oranges, sliced	¾ cup	orange juice
2 cups	orange juice	½ cup	honey
		1 tsp.	turmeric
YELLOW BBQ SAUCE		1 tsp.	ground cumin
2	yellow bell peppers, seeded and diced	1 tsp.	black pepper
		½ tsp.	cayenne pepper
1	small yellow onion, finely chopped		Salt to taste
4 cloves	garlic, minced		

1. Preheat oven to 325°F.

2. Using a sharp knife, score the membrane on the backside of the ribs in a diamond pattern. Rub with the BBQ spice, pressing the seasoning into the meat. Lay the ribs meat side down in a roasting pan. Lay 3 to 4 slices of orange on the back of each rib. Pour in orange juice. Cover tightly with lid or foil.

3. Braise ribs for 2 to 2½ hours or until tender. Let cool slightly.

4. Meanwhile, prepare the sauce. In a medium saucepan, combine the yellow peppers, onion, garlic, mustard, vinegar, orange juice, honey, turmeric, cumin, black pepper and cayenne. Bring to a boil, stirring. Reduce heat to medium-low and simmer, stirring occasionally, for 20 to 30 minutes or until reduced by one-third. Season with salt. In a blender, purée the mixture until smooth. Let cool.

5. Preheat grill to medium-high.

6. Grill ribs for 6 to 8 minutes per side, basting with sauce.

7. Cut between every third rib and serve.

SERVES 4 TO 6

Pineapple Juice Boiled Spareribs with Sweet-and-Sour Plum Sauce

When you boil your ribs in pineapple juice, you don't need to marinate the meat first. The high acidity of the pineapple juice tenderizes the ribs.

2 racks	pork spareribs (each 2 to 3 lb.)	**SWEET-AND-SOUR PLUM SAUCE**	
8 cups	pineapple juice	½ cup	corn syrup
6 cloves	garlic	½ cup	plum sauce
2 tsp.	ground cumin	½ cup	rice wine vinegar
2 tsp.	black pepper	2 tbsp.	ketchup
1 tsp.	cinnamon	1 tbsp.	minced fresh ginger
		1 tbsp.	soy sauce
			Salt and pepper

1. Using a sharp knife, score the membrane on the backside of the ribs in a diamond pattern.

2. In a large pot bring the pineapple juice and garlic to a boil. Add the spareribs, reduce heat to medium-low, cover and simmer for 2 hours or until tender. Remove ribs from pot and cool slightly. Discard braising liquid.

3. Meanwhile, prepare the sauce. In a medium saucepan combine the corn syrup, plum sauce, vinegar, ketchup, ginger and soy sauce. Bring to a boil, stirring. Reduce heat to medium-low and simmer for 15 minutes, stirring occasionally. Season to taste with salt and pepper. Let cool.

4. Preheat grill to medium-high.

5. In a small bowl combine the cumin, pepper and cinnamon. Rub ribs with seasoning mixture. Grill for 8 to 10 minutes per side, basting liberally with sauce.

6. Cut between every third rib and serve.

SERVES 4

Jalapeño Beer Braised Back Ribs

These ribs are a favourite of my golfing buddy Chris Harper. Chris is a cigar aficionado with a penchant for spicy ribs.

1	large yellow onion, sliced	2 tbsp.	Bone Dust BBQ Spice (page 97)
4	jalapeño peppers, sliced	3	limes, sliced
4 cloves	garlic, minced	2 cans	beer
4 racks	baby back ribs (each 1½ lb.)	2 cups	gourmet BBQ sauce

1. Preheat oven to 325°F.

2. In a bowl combine the onion, jalapeño peppers and garlic. Spread the mixture in a roasting pan.

3. Using a sharp knife, score the membrane on the backside of the ribs in a diamond pattern. Rub with the BBQ spice, pressing the seasoning into the meat. Lay the ribs meat side down on top of the onion mixture. Lay 3 or 4 lime slices on the back of each rib. Pour in beer. Cover tightly with lid or foil.

4. Braise ribs for 2 to 2½ hours or until tender. Let cool slightly. Remove ribs from pan and set aside.

5. Pour onion/beer mixture into a large saucepan and bring to a boil. Reduce liquid by half, stirring occasionally. Add the BBQ sauce. Return to boil, then remove from heat. In a blender or food processor, purée the sauce until smooth.

6. Meanwhile, preheat grill to medium-high.

7. Grill ribs for 6 to 8 minutes per side, basting with sauce.

8. Cut between every third rib and serve.

SERVES 4 TO 6

Bourbon Smoked St. Louis Spareribs

Sweet bourbon makes a great addition to any BBQ sauce. Ask your butcher to prepare the St. Louis ribs by removing the soft bone brisket.

4 racks	St. Louis–style spareribs (each 2 to 2½ lb.)	**BOURBON BBQ SAUCE**	
2 cups	bourbon	2 cups	hickory smoke–flavoured BBQ sauce
2 cups	water	½ cup	bourbon
½ cup	brown sugar	¼ cup	molasses
¼ cup	salt	2 tbsp.	vegetable oil
	Hickory smoking chips	1 tbsp.	Worcestershire sauce
¼ cup	Bone Dust BBQ Spice (page 97)	1 tsp.	black pepper
		1 tsp.	mustard powder
		1	small yellow onion, diced
		4 cloves	garlic, minced
		Dash	hot sauce
			Salt to taste

1. Using a sharp knife, score the membrane on the backside of the ribs in a diamond pattern. Place the ribs in a large pan. Stir together the bourbon, water, sugar and salt. Pour over the ribs, turning to coat. Marinate, covered and refrigerated, for 4 to 6 hours or overnight.

2. Prepare smoker as per smoking instructions (page 109). Soak hickory wood chips in water while coals are heating.

3. Remove ribs from marinade, reserving marinade. Rub ribs with the BBQ spice, pressing the seasoning into the meat.

4. Place ribs in smoker and add wood chips to coals. Close the lid and smoke ribs for 4 hours, basting every hour with reserved marinade and replenishing coals and wood chips as needed.

5. Meanwhile, make the sauce. In a medium saucepan, combine the BBQ sauce, bourbon, molasses, oil, Worcestershire sauce, pepper, mustard powder, onion, garlic and hot sauce. Bring to a boil, stirring. Reduce heat and simmer for 15 minutes. Remove from heat. Season with salt.

6. Preheat grill to medium-high.

7. Remove ribs from smoker. Grill ribs for 10 to 12 minutes per side, basting liberally with sauce.

8. Cut between every third rib and serve.

SERVES 4 TO 6

Root Beer Ribs with Drive-In BBQ Sauce

When I was a kid, a Teen Burger and a frosty mug of root beer was an awesome treat. Inspired by that combination, I developed this funky recipe using root beer.

4 racks	pork baby back ribs (each 1½ lb.)	**DRIVE-IN BBQ SAUCE**	
6 tbsp.	Bone Dust BBQ Spice (page 97)	1 cup	ketchup
		½ cup	brown sugar
2	onions, sliced	½ cup	root beer
4 cloves	garlic, smashed	2 tbsp.	chopped fresh cilantro
4	bottles or cans (each 375 mL) A&W Root Beer	2 tbsp.	water
		1 tbsp.	Worcestershire sauce
1 tbsp.	root beer essence or vanilla		Salt to taste

1. Preheat oven to 325°F.

2. Using a sharp knife, score the membrane on the backside of the ribs in a diamond pattern. Season the ribs with the BBQ spice, pressing the seasoning into the meat.

3. Spread the onions and garlic in a roasting pan. Lay the ribs meat side down on top of the onion mixture.

4. Stir together the root beer and root beer essence; pour over the ribs. Cover tightly with lid or foil.

5. Braise for 2 to 2½ hours or until the meat is tender. Let cool slightly.

6. Meanwhile, make the sauce. Whisk together the ketchup, brown sugar, root beer, cilantro, water, Worcestershire sauce and salt.

7. Preheat grill to medium-high.

8. Grill ribs for 6 to 8 minutes per side or until lightly charred, basting frequently with the sauce.

9. Cut between every third rib and serve.

SERVES 4 TO 6

Honey Garlic Cinnamon Spareribs

For this recipe, you can never have enough garlic. The more, the better.

2 racks	pork spareribs (each 2 to 3 lb.)	**HONEY GARLIC SAUCE**	
¼ cup	Indonesian Cinnamon Rub (page 100)	1 cup	honey
		½ cup	pineapple juice
8 cloves	garlic, minced	¼ cup	sesame seeds
2 cups	water	¼ cup	soy sauce
		¼ cup	rice vinegar
		1 tsp.	cinnamon
		12 cloves	garlic, minced
			Salt and freshly ground black pepper

1. Preheat oven to 325°F.

2. Using a sharp knife, score the membrane on the backside of the ribs in a diamond pattern. Season the spareribs with the Indonesian rub, pressing the spices into the meat. Place the ribs in a large roasting pan and add garlic and water. Cover tightly with lid or foil.

3. Braise for 2 to 2½ hours or until the meat is tender. Let cool slightly.

4. Meanwhile, make the sauce by mixing together the honey, pineapple juice, sesame seeds, soy sauce, vinegar, cinnamon and garlic. Season to taste with salt and pepper. Bring to a boil. Remove from heat and keep warm.

5. Preheat grill to medium-high.

6. Grill ribs for 6 to 8 minutes per side or until lightly charred, basting frequently with the sauce.

7. Cut between every third rib and toss with remaining honey garlic sauce.

SERVES 4 TO 6

Char Siu Country-Style Pork Ribs

Char siu is Chinese sweet roasted pork. This Chinese-style BBQ marinade is traditionally very red in colour because of the red food colouring in the sauce. I have included food colouring in the recipe, but you do not have to use it.

2 racks	country-style pork ribs (each 1 to 1½ lb.)	¼ cup	hoisin sauce
¼ cup	Indonesian Cinnamon Rub (page 100)	¼ cup	honey
½ cup	brown sugar	4 cloves	garlic, minced
½ cup	soy sauce	1 to 2 tsp.	salt
		¼ tsp.	red food colouring (optional)

1. Rub the ribs with the Indonesian rub, pressing the seasoning into the meat. Place in a large roasting pan.

2. Mix together the brown sugar, soy sauce, hoisin sauce, honey, garlic, salt and food colouring. Pour over the ribs, turning to coat. Marinate, covered and refrigerated, for 24 hours.

3. Preheat grill to medium-high.

4. Remove ribs from marinade, discarding marinade. Grill for 40 to 50 minutes or until a meat thermometer reads 160°F.

5. Thinly slice and serve.

SERVES 6 TO 8

Barbecued Back Ribs with Maple Bacon BBQ Sauce

Serve these ribs with Cheesy Macaroni Salad (page 36).

---

4 racks	pork baby back ribs (each 1½ lb.)		1 cup	applesauce
2 tbsp.	Bone Dust BBQ Spice (page 97)		½ cup	maple syrup
2	lemons, sliced		¼ cup	cider vinegar
2 cups	apple juice		2 tbsp.	hot sauce
			2 tbsp.	Worcestershire sauce
MAPLE BACON BBQ SAUCE			2 tsp.	celery salt
8 slices	bacon, diced		1½ tsp.	liquid smoke
6 cloves	garlic, minced		1 tsp.	mustard powder
1	large onion, diced		¼ tsp.	cayenne pepper
1½ cups	ketchup			Salt

---

1. Preheat oven to 325°F.

2. Score the membrane on the backside of the ribs in a diamond pattern. Rub with the BBQ spice, pressing the seasoning into the meat. Lay the ribs meat side down in a roasting pan. Lay 3 or 4 lemon slices on the back of each rib. Pour in apple juice. Cover tightly with lid or foil. Braise for 2 to 2½ hours or until tender. Let cool slightly.

3. Meanwhile, prepare the sauce. In a medium saucepan over medium heat, fry the bacon until it is half-cooked. Drain off all but 3 tbsp. of the drippings. Add the garlic and onions. Fry, stirring, until the onions are tender and golden brown. Add the ketchup, applesauce, maple syrup, vinegar, hot sauce, Worcestershire sauce, celery salt, liquid smoke, mustard powder and cayenne. Bring to a boil, reduce heat to low and simmer, stirring occasionally, for 15 minutes. Season with salt to taste. Set aside.

4. Preheat grill to medium-high.

5. Remove ribs from pan, discarding braising liquid. Grill ribs for 6 to 8 minutes per side or until lightly charred, basting with sauce.

6. Cut between every third rib and toss with remaining sauce.

SERVES 4 TO 6

Honey Hoisin–Glazed Grilled Spareribs

These ribs require a generous amount of glazing during the final 30 minutes of grilling. The more baste, the stickier and tastier the ribs will be.

---

2 racks	pork spareribs (each 2 to 3 lb.)	2 tbsp.	chopped fresh rosemary
½ cup	Miami Spice Love Paste (page 102)	2 tbsp.	rice wine vinegar
		1 tbsp.	chopped fresh ginger
2 to 4 cans	ginger ale	1 tbsp.	sesame seeds
		1 tsp.	mustard powder
HONEY HOISIN GLAZE		1 tsp.	cracked black pepper
1 cup	hoisin sauce	3	green onions, finely chopped
1 cup	honey		Salt to taste
½ cup	orange juice		

---

1. Using a sharp knife, score the membrane on the backside of the ribs in a diamond pattern. Rub with the Miami Spice Love Paste, pressing the seasoning into the meat. Lay ribs in a roasting pan and pour in enough ginger ale to cover. Marinate, covered and refrigerated, for 4 to 6 hours or overnight.

2. Prepare the glaze. In a medium bowl, combine the hoisin sauce, honey, orange juice, rosemary, vinegar, ginger, sesame seeds, mustard powder, black pepper and green onions. Season with salt and set aside.

3. Preheat grill to medium.

4. Remove ribs from roasting pan, discarding liquid. Grill for 90 minutes, turning the ribs every 15 minutes. During the last 30 minutes of grilling, baste liberally with the honey hoisin glaze.

5. Cut between every third rib and serve.

SERVES 4

Devil's Brewed Roast Chicken with White Trash BBQ Sauce, p. 184

Root Beer Ribs with Drive-In BBQ Sauce, p. 116

Cedar-Planked Haddock Stuffed with Crab, Shrimp and Cheddar Cheese, p. 198

Margarita Wings, p. 39

Shrimp Parfait with Lucifer Cocktail Sauce, p. 52

Rocketship 7 Peanut Butter and Jelly Steaks, p. 146

Cinnamon-Skewered Scallops with Brown Sugar and Peach-Orange Salsa, p. 205

The Burger Is Better with Butter, p. 76

Moroccan Pomegranate-Glazed Back Ribs

You'll find pomegranate molasses in specialty or Middle Eastern food shops.

4 racks	pork baby back ribs (each 1½ lb.)	½ cup	honey
2 tbsp.	Bone Dust BBQ Spice (page 97)	¼ cup	lemon juice
2	oranges, sliced	1 tbsp.	chopped fresh cilantro
2 cups	orange juice	1 tbsp.	chopped fresh parsley
		1 tbsp.	chopped fresh mint
POMEGRANATE GLAZE		3	green onions, finely chopped
2 tbsp.	olive oil	1 tbsp.	sesame seeds
1 tbsp.	chopped fresh ginger	1 tsp.	ground cumin
4 cloves	garlic, minced	1 tsp.	black pepper
1 cup	pomegranate molasses	¼ tsp.	nutmeg
			Salt to taste

1. Preheat oven to 325°F.

2. Using a sharp knife, score the membrane on the backside of the ribs in a diamond pattern. Rub with the BBQ spice, pressing the seasoning into the meat. Lay the ribs meat side down in a roasting pan. Lay 3 or 4 orange slices on the back of each rib. Pour in orange juice. Cover tightly with lid or foil.

3. Braise for 2 to 2½ hours or until tender. Let cool slightly.

4. Meanwhile, prepare the pomegranate glaze. In a medium saucepan over medium heat, heat the oil. Sauté the ginger and garlic, stirring, for 2 to 3 minutes or until tender. Add the pomegranate molasses, honey, lemon juice, cilantro, parsley, mint and green onions. Bring to a boil, stirring occasionally. Reduce heat and simmer, stirring, for 10 minutes. Remove from heat and stir in sesame seeds, cumin, pepper, nutmeg and salt.

5. Preheat grill to medium.

6. Remove ribs from roasting pan, discarding liquid. Grill for 10 to 12 minutes per side, basting with glaze.

7. Cut between every third rib and serve.

SERVES 4 TO 6

Mahogany Glazed Back Rib Tail Pieces

This classic Chinese glaze makes ribs rich in colour and flavour. Mildly spiced, these appetizer rib pieces will draw crowds to the table.

6 cups	pineapple juice		¼ cup	brown sugar
2 lb.	pork back rib tail pieces		¼ cup	soy sauce
2 tbsp.	Licorice Rub (page 103)		¼ cup	dry sherry
			¼ cup	rice wine vinegar
MAHOGANY GLAZE			8 cloves	garlic, minced
¾ cup	plum sauce		1 tbsp.	minced fresh ginger
½ cup	hoisin sauce		3	green onions, finely chopped

1. Pour the pineapple juice into a steamer pot and bring to a boil. Rub the back rib tail pieces with the Licorice Rub and place in top portion of steamer. Steam ribs for 45 to 60 minutes or until tender.

2. Meanwhile, prepare the glaze. In a bowl whisk together the plum sauce, hoisin sauce, soy sauce, sherry, vinegar, brown sugar, garlic, ginger and green onions. Set aside.

3. Preheat grill to medium-high.

4. Grill rib pieces for 5 to 6 minutes per side, basting generously with glaze.

5. Serve immediately.

SERVES 2 TO 4

Tandoori Back Ribs

If you want to save a little time, buy a commercial tandoori paste, readily available in specialty food shops or in the ethnic section of grocery stores.

TANDOORI MARINADE			
2 cups	plain yogurt	1 tbsp.	cinnamon
1 tbsp.	lemon juice	1 tbsp.	black pepper
2 tsp.	salt	1 tsp.	ground cloves
¼ cup	paprika	¼ cup	clarified butter
2 tbsp.	ground cumin	1 tbsp.	minced fresh ginger
1 tbsp.	cayenne pepper	6 cloves	garlic, minced
1 tbsp.	ground coriander		
1 tbsp.	ground cardamom	4 racks	pork baby back ribs (each 1½ lb.)

1. In a large bowl blend the yogurt, lemon juice and salt. Set aside.

2. In a small bowl combine the paprika, cumin, cayenne, coriander, cardamom, cinnamon, black pepper and cloves.

3. In a frying pan, heat the clarified butter over medium heat until hot but not smoking. Add the ginger and garlic; sauté, stirring, for 1 to 2 minutes or until tender. Add the spice blend and fry, stirring, for 30 seconds to 1 minute, being careful not to burn the spices. Transfer the spices to the yogurt and whisk until fully incorporated.

4. Using a sharp knife, score the membrane on the backside of the ribs in a diamond pattern. Lay ribs in a large dish. Pour tandoori marinade over ribs, turning to coat. Marinate, covered and refrigerated, for 4 to 6 hours or overnight.

5. Preheat oven to 350°F.

6. Remove ribs from marinade, reserving marinade. Place ribs on a rack in a roasting pan. Roast ribs for 1 to 1¼ hours or until tender.

7. Preheat grill to medium-high.

8. Grill ribs for 8 to 10 minutes per side, basting with tandoori marinade.

9. Cut between every third rib and serve.

SERVES 4

The Boneless Rib (a.k.a. Beer-Marinated Boneless Pork Rib with Beer BBQ Sauce)

Ribs are delicious but are mostly bone. This boneless rib is a pork loin cut into three lengthwise, slowly braised and then grilled. All meat and all tender — no bones about it.

1	boneless pork loin	
	(3 to 4 lb. and about 1 foot long)	
½ cup	Bone Dust BBQ Spice (page 97)	
2	lemons, thinly sliced	
2 bottles	beer	

BEER BBQ SAUCE

1½ cups	hickory smoke–flavoured BBQ sauce
1 cup	beer
½ cup	brown sugar
½ cup	ketchup
1 tbsp.	lemon juice
2 tsp.	Bone Dust BBQ Spice (page 97)
	Salt to taste

1. Cut the pork loin lengthwise into 3 equal pieces. The pieces should look similar to a back rib but without the bones. Rub the pork with the BBQ spice, pushing the spices into the meat. Place pork in a roasting pan. Lay 3 or 4 lemon slices on each "rib." Pour the beer over the pork. Marinate, covered and refrigerated, for 2 to 4 hours.

2. Preheat oven to 375°F.

3. Cover ribs tightly with lid or foil. Braise for 1½ hours or until tender. Let cool in the beer.

4. While the ribs are cooling make the sauce. Whisk together BBQ sauce, beer, brown sugar, ketchup, lemon juice, BBQ spice and salt.

5. Preheat grill to medium-high.

6. Remove pork from the marinade, discarding marinade. Grill "ribs" for 3 to 4 minutes per side or until lightly charred, basting liberally with sauce.

7. Slice pork into 1-inch-thick slices to resemble ribs. Transfer to a serving platter and serve with remaining sauce for dipping.

SERVES 8

BBQ Beef Short Ribs

Braising these ribs slowly makes them fall-off-the-bone tender.

4 lb.	beef short ribs, cut into 6-inch lengths	1 cup	BBQ sauce
½ cup	Great Canadian Steak Spice (page 97)	1 cup	chili sauce
		¼ cup	honey
¼ cup	vegetable oil	3 tbsp.	sambal chili paste
4 cloves	garlic, chopped	2 tbsp.	Worcestershire sauce
1 can	beer	1 tbsp.	chopped fresh cilantro
		1	large onion, sliced

1. Preheat oven to 325°F.

2. In a large bowl toss the beef ribs with the steak spice and vegetable oil.

3. In another bowl whisk together the garlic, beer, BBQ sauce, chili sauce, honey, sambal, Worcestershire sauce and cilantro. Stir in the onion and set aside.

4. In a frying pan over medium-high heat, sear the ribs for 2 to 3 minutes per side or until lightly charred. Transfer ribs to a roasting pan. Pour the sauce over the ribs and stir to coat evenly. Cover with lid or foil. Braise for 1½ to 2 hours or until the meat is tender and can be easily separated from the bone.

5. Transfer ribs to a platter, reserving pan liquids, and let cool for 15 to 20 minutes.

6. Meanwhile, preheat grill to medium-high.

7. Grill ribs for 5 to 6 minutes per side or until lightly charred and tender, basting with pan liquids.

SERVES 6 TO 8

Refrigerator Short Ribs

I first cooked these ribs with my dad in our hometown of Paris, Ontario. We were on our own for a few weeks, and Dad brought home some beef short ribs. After a little research on how to prepare them, we dug around in the fridge for some ingredients and came up with this recipe.

1 cup	all-purpose flour		2 stalks	celery, diced
1 tsp.	salt		1	green bell pepper, thinly sliced
1 tsp.	black pepper		1 cup	prepared yellow mustard
1 tsp.	mustard powder		½ cup	corn syrup
½ tsp.	cayenne pepper		½ cup	malt vinegar
4 lb.	beef short ribs		¼ cup	chopped fresh parsley
¼ cup	vegetable oil		1½ cups	water
2	large Spanish onions, sliced			Salt
8 cloves	garlic, minced			

1. Preheat oven to 325°F.

2. In a bowl blend the flour, salt, pepper, mustard powder and cayenne. Roll the short ribs in the seasoned flour, shaking off any excess flour.

3. In a large frying pan over medium-high heat, heat the oil. Fry the ribs until golden brown on all sides, about 3 minutes per side. Transfer ribs to a roasting pan.

4. In a bowl combine the onions, garlic, celery and green pepper. Spread mixture over the ribs. In the same bowl stir together the prepared mustard, corn syrup, vinegar, parsley and water. Season to taste with salt. Pour over ribs. Cover tightly with lid or foil. Braise for 1½ to 2 hours or until tender.

5. Transfer ribs to a platter, reserving mustard-onion mixture, and let cool for 15 to 20 minutes.

6. Meanwhile, preheat grill to medium-high.

7. Grill ribs for 5 to 6 minutes per side or until lightly charred and tender, basting with pan liquids. Serve with remaining mustard-onion mixture.

SERVES 6 TO 8

Maui Beef Ribs

Cut from the ends of a beef rib roast and the plate, these short ribs are made up of flat rib bones with layers of meat and fat. Ask your butcher to prepare the short ribs Maui, or Miami, style. These ribs will be about ½-inch thick and 1½ inches wide and have 5 rib bones. Marinate for at least 6 hours and then grill them quickly over high heat.

¼ cup	vegetable oil		2	shallots, diced
¼ cup	brown sugar		4	green onions, finely chopped
¼ cup	dry sherry		1 stalk	lemon grass, pale green part only, smashed
¼ cup	balsamic vinegar			and finely chopped
2 tbsp.	chopped fresh ginger		2 tsp.	cracked black pepper
2 tbsp.	molasses		1 tsp.	salt
1 tbsp.	sesame oil		4 lb.	beef short ribs, cut across the bones
6 cloves	garlic, minced			½-inch thick (about 15 to 20 pieces)

1. In a glass dish large enough to hold the ribs, combine the vegetable oil, sugar, sherry, vinegar, ginger, molasses, sesame oil, garlic, shallots, green onions, lemon grass, pepper and salt.

2. Add the ribs, turning to coat. Marinate, covered and refrigerated, for 4 to 6 hours or overnight.

3. Preheat grill to high.

4. Remove ribs from marinade, reserving marinade. Grill for 2 to 3 minutes per side, basting liberally with reserved marinade.

SERVES 4 TO 6

Drumheller Beef Ribs

Drumheller, in the Badlands of Alberta, is the home of "dinosaur graveyards" — an archeological site that has uncovered dinosaur bones from millions of years ago. My "dinosaur bones" recipe calls for prime rib of beef. Allow a half rack of ribs per person. These delicious ribs are slowly smoked over hickory wood chips and basted with a smoky onion BBQ sauce.

2 racks	prime rib of beef back ribs (each 5 lb.)		8 cloves	garlic, chopped
¼ cup	Bone Dust BBQ Spice (page 97)		2 cups	hickory smoke–flavoured BBQ sauce
	Hickory smoking chips		¼ cup	brown sugar
			¼ cup	dark rum
SMOKY ONION BBQ SAUCE			1 tbsp.	chopped fresh rosemary
3 tbsp.	vegetable oil		1 tsp.	liquid smoke
2	onions, sliced			Salt and pepper to taste

Tip

Ask your butcher to cut the racks of beef ribs in half lengthwise (across the bones) to give you narrow racks of ribs similar to pork spareribs.

1. Rub the racks with the BBQ spice, pressing the seasoning into the meat. Cover and marinate at room temperature for 30 minutes.

2. To prepare the sauce, heat the oil in a large saucepan. Sauté the onions and garlic, stirring, until caramelized. Add the BBQ sauce, sugar, rum, rosemary and liquid smoke. Bring to a boil; reduce heat and simmer for 15 minutes, stirring occasionally. Season with salt and pepper and set aside.

3. Prepare smoker as per smoking instructions (page 109). Soak hickory wood chips in water while coals are heating.

4. Add wood chips to coals and place ribs in smoker. Close the lid and smoke ribs for 3 to 4 hours, basting every hour with sauce and replenishing coals and wood chips as needed.

5. Remove ribs from smoker and glaze with extra sauce.

6. Serve immediately with lots of wet cloths and napkins.

SERVES 4

Grilled Lamb Ribs with Sweet Jalapeño BBQ Glaze

Lamb ribs are tender and delicious. You will not always find them in grocery stores, so special-order them through your specialty meat shop or butcher.

8 racks	lamb ribs (each 8 to 10 oz. trimmed)	**SWEET JALAPEÑO BBQ GLAZE**	
¼ cup	Licorice Rub (page 103)	1 cup	jalapeño jelly
1	large onion, sliced	3 tbsp.	cider vinegar
2 tbsp.	chopped garlic	2 tbsp.	lemon juice
2	lemons, thinly sliced	1 tbsp.	chopped fresh cilantro
2 cups	water		Black pepper to taste

1. Preheat oven to 325°F.

2. With a sharp knife, score the lamb ribs on both sides in a diamond pattern. Season the ribs with the Licorice Rub, pressing the spices into the meat.

3. Place the onion, garlic, lemon slices and water in a large roasting pan. Arrange ribs on top of the onion mixture. Cover tightly with lid or foil. Bake for 1½ hours or until tender. Let cool.

4. Meanwhile, make the glaze. In a small saucepan, stir together the jalapeño jelly, vinegar and lemon juice. Bring to a boil and whisk until smooth. Remove from heat and stir in cilantro and pepper. Let cool.

5. Preheat grill to medium-high.

6. Grill ribs, basting with glaze, for 4 to 5 minutes per side.

7. Cut between every second bone and serve with grilled potatoes, if desired.

SERVES 4

Thai Marinated Lamb Ribs with Spicy Peanut Sauce

This is my friend Chef Wendy Baskerville's recipe for grilled lamb ribs with a spicy peanut sauce. Wendy prepared these tasty ribs for me when she owned Babette's Feast Catering in Toronto.

½ cup	coconut milk	**SPICY PEANUT SAUCE**	
1 stalk	lemon grass, pale green part only, smashed and chopped	2 tbsp.	vegetable oil
		2	shallots, diced
3	limes, juiced	2 cloves	garlic, minced
2	small spicy Thai green chilies	1 tbsp.	minced fresh ginger
1 tbsp.	chopped fresh ginger	1 cup	crunchy peanut butter
6 cloves	garlic, minced	1 cup	coconut milk
2 tbsp.	brown sugar	½ cup	dry sherry
2 tbsp.	vegetable oil	1	lime, zested and juiced
1 tsp.	cracked black pepper	¼ cup	rice wine vinegar
8 racks	lamb ribs	1 tbsp.	chopped fresh cilantro
	(each 8 to 10 oz. trimmed)	1 tbsp.	sambal chili paste

Tip

Lamb ribs can be hard to find, so you may need to order them from your butcher. Cook the ribs over medium to medium-low heat; you want to cook them slowly to allow all the flavours to permeate the meat and to keep the meat from burning and drying out.

1. In a glass dish large enough to hold the lamb, stir together well the coconut milk, lemon grass, lime juice, chilies, ginger, garlic, sugar, oil and pepper.

2. With a sharp knife, score the lamb ribs on both sides in a diamond pattern. Add ribs to marinade, turning to coat. Marinate, covered and refrigerated, for 4 to 6 hours.

3. Meanwhile, make the sauce. Heat the vegetable oil in a medium saucepan over medium heat. Sauté the shallots, garlic and ginger, stirring, until tender. Add the peanut butter, coconut milk and sherry, stirring until smooth. Add the lime zest and juice, vinegar, sambal and cilantro. Bring to a low boil, stirring to prevent sticking, and simmer for 5 to 10 minutes, stirring occasionally. Let cool.

4. Preheat grill to medium.

5. Remove ribs from marinade, reserving marinade. Grill for 20 to 30 minutes per side or until tender, basting with marinade.

6. Meanwhile, reheat peanut sauce.

7. Remove ribs from grill. Cut between every second rib and serve with warmed peanut sauce for dipping.

SERVES 4

Tender Loins

Steak Basics

Beef

Steak Cuts

Tenderloin

Of all of the steak cuts, the tenderloin is the most tender. The tenderloin comes from the short loin of beef; it lies between the rib and the sirloin and never really does anything but lie there and be tender. The tenderloin may be cooked whole or cut into wonderfully tender steaks. Be careful not to overcook this cut. It does not have a lot of fat, so it tends to dry out and become tough the more it cooks.

Striploin

The striploin steak is one of the most popular cuts of beef. It comes from the top loin muscle in the short loin of beef. It is best grilled to medium-rare and is often served with a peppercorn sauce. This steak is known by many names, the most popular being the New York strip steak and Kansas City steak. A bone-in striploin steak is known as a shell steak.

Rib-Eye Steak

This steak is cut from between the rib and chuck section. The bone-in rib steak is also known as the cowboy steak. The rib steak is an extremely tender cut of beef. This steak is heavily marbled with fat, giving it maximum flavour. It is best to grill this steak to medium-rare, which allows the internal fat to melt and bring out the natural juices and flavour.

T-Bone Steak

This steak is named after the shape of its bone, a large T that separates the striploin from the small tenderloin. Cut from the centre of the short loin, this is a large steak, often best shared, but if you're truly hungry it is a real meal for one. I like to serve this steak with lots of sautéed onions and mushrooms and topped with crumbled blue cheese.

Porterhouse Steak

A porterhouse steak is cut from the large end of the short loin and also has the same T-shaped bone as the T-bone. It has a larger tenderloin portion and is truly a meal for two — it's sometimes called the king of steaks. It is often cut into 2-inch-thick portions weighing approximately 36 oz. Rub this steak with garlic, black pepper and fresh rosemary and grill it over medium-high heat.

Sirloin Steak

Cut from the area between the short loin and round, the sirloin has three main muscles. Cut into steaks, they are quite flavourful but require marinating to make them a little more tender. A teriyaki marinade is the most popular marinade used on sirloin steaks.

Flank Steak

The flank steak comes from the lower hind region of beef. It is a tougher cut of steak that requires marinating to make it tender. As it does not have a lot of internal fat, be careful not to overcook it. Marinated in an Asian marinade, this steak will have great flavour.
It is best sliced thinly when served and is a great steak for a salad or steak sandwich.

Hanger Steak

The hanger steak hangs between the rib cage and loin cage. Hanger steaks have a little stronger flavour than regular steaks and need to be very fresh. Ask your butcher for this tender cut of beef, which isn't usually found in grocery stores. Marinate it with stronger-flavoured herbs and spices and lots of garlic. It is best cooked rare to medium and sliced thinly.

Cooking Steak

How Do You Like Your Steak Cooked?

Blue Rare: A blue rare steak is quickly charred on the outside and barely cooked on the inside. For best results, bring the steak to room temperature before cooking.

Rare: A rare steak has a cool red centre.

Medium-Rare: A medium-rare steak has a warm red centre.

Medium: A medium steak has a pink centre and the juices are clear.

Medium-Well: A medium-well steak has a hot pink centre and the juices are clear.

Well-Done: A well-done steak is grey throughout without any trace of pink and the juices are clear.

Super Well-Done: This steak is weighted with a brick until heavily charred on the outside and without any trace of pink and no juices inside.

How to Test for Doneness for Your Perfect Steak

The best way to test for doneness on a steak is to use a meat thermometer.

Blue rare	130°F
Rare	130 to 140°F
Medium-rare	140 to 145°F
Medium	145 to 150°F
Medium-well	150 to 160°F
Well-done	160 to 170°F
Super well done	170°F plus

The next best method to test for doneness is the Hand Touch Method. Shake one hand loose so that it is completely relaxed. With your other hand, touch the soft fleshy part of your relaxed hand below the base of your thumb. This soft texture is similar to the texture of a blue rare to rare steak.

Now touch your thumb and forefinger together and again touch the base of your thumb. This texture is similar to a medium-rare steak.

Next, touch your thumb to your middle finger. This firmer texture is similar to the texture of a medium steak.

Next, touch your thumb to your fourth finger. The semi-firm texture at the base of your thumb is similar to a medium-well steak.

Lastly, touch your thumb to your pinky finger. The very firm texture at the base of your thumb is similar to a well-done steak.

This method of testing a steak is relatively easy and you will never find yourself looking for a thermometer while grilling.

One last note: *never* use a knife to cut the meat to test for doneness. Cutting the steak lets all the natural juices escape, leaving you with a dry and tasteless piece of meat.

Dad's Wheelbarrow Steak

As a kid I never wanted to have any of my friends over for a BBQ. This was not because of the food that was served (that was always outstanding) but because my dad had the most embarrassing barbecue in town. After our real charcoal grill rusted out and the legs fell off and that last juicy steak hit the dirt, my dad decided that he'd be thrifty and use his wheelbarrow. Well, life was never the same. So this recipe is dedicated to my dad, whose unorthodox grill still cooked a mean steak.

1	sirloin steak (about 4 lb. and 3 inches thick)	¼ cup	ketchup
¼ cup	Malabar Pepper Rub (page 96)	2 tbsp.	chopped fresh herbs (such as parsley, sage, rosemary)
8 cloves	garlic, minced	1 tbsp.	Worcestershire sauce
1 cup	dry red wine		Salt to taste
¼ cup	vegetable oil		

1. Rub the steak with the Malabar Pepper Rub, pressing the seasoning into the meat.

2. In a glass dish large enough to hold the steak, whisk together the garlic, wine, vegetable oil, ketchup, herbs, Worcestershire sauce and salt. Add steak, turning once to coat. Marinate, covered and refrigerated, for 6 hours or overnight.

3. Preheat wheelbarrow to high.

4. Remove steak from marinade, reserving marinade. Grill steak for 10 to 12 minutes per side for medium, basting with marinade. Remove from the grill and let rest for 10 minutes.

5. Thinly slice the steak across the grain and serve with prepared horseradish and steak sauce.

SERVES 4 TO 6

Tip

When buying a large steak, choose one that is a uniform thickness. I like a relatively thick steak, about 3 to 4 inches. Buy a top-quality cut of sirloin, meaning AAA Canadian Beef or USDA Prime or Certified Black Angus. The better the quality of beef, the tastier your steak will be.

Classic Bacon-Wrapped Filet with Sauce Béarnaise

The reason a lot of people wrap a filet in bacon is that the bacon fat adds the bulk of flavour to the filet. The bacon also helps to retain the steak's moisture, keeping it tender.

I like to precook my bacon to prevent too much grill flare-up.

6 to			4	egg yolks
12 slices	thick bacon		2 tbsp.	dry white wine
6	beef tenderloin filets (each 8 oz.)		1 tbsp.	dry sherry
2 tbsp.	Great Canadian Steak Spice		1 cup +	
	(page 97)		2 tbsp.	clarified butter
			1 tbsp.	chopped fresh tarragon
SAUCE BÉARNAISE			1 tbsp.	Dijon mustard
¼ cup	cider vinegar		1 tsp.	lemon juice
2 sprigs	fresh tarragon		Dash	hot sauce
1	small shallot, diced		Dash	Worcestershire sauce
2 tbsp.	water			Salt and pepper to taste
4	black peppercorns			

1. Fry the bacon for 2 to 3 minutes per side or until slightly done. (You do not want to fry the bacon crisp or you will not be able to wrap it around the filets.) Remove from pan and pat dry with paper towels to remove excess fat. Set aside.

2. Rub the filets all over with the steak spice, pressing the seasoning into the meat.

3. Wrap each filet with a slice of bacon. Use a half slice extra if the bacon does not quite make it all the way around. Secure with a toothpick and set aside to marinate at room temperature for 30 minutes.

4. Meanwhile, make the sauce. In a small saucepan bring the vinegar, tarragon sprigs, shallot, water and peppercorns to a boil. Reduce heat and simmer for 3 to 4 minutes or until the liquid has reduced by half. Remove from heat and strain. Discard solids and let the liquid cool.

5. In a medium bowl whisk the egg yolks, white wine, sherry and cooled vinegar mixture. Place over a pot of simmering water and whisk constantly until the mixture is thick enough to form a ribbon when drizzled from the whisk. Be careful not to turn this into scrambled eggs. Remove from heat.

6. Whisking constantly, slowly add the clarified butter a little at a time until all the butter has been absorbed. Season with chopped tarragon, mustard, lemon juice, hot sauce, Worcestershire sauce, salt and pepper. Remove from heat and keep warm over the hot water.

7. Preheat grill to medium-high.

8. Grill beef for 4 to 5 minutes per side for medium and until the bacon is crispy.

9. Remove toothpicks and serve filets drizzled with sauce Béarnaise.

SERVES 6

Oscar's Steak Oscar

Classic steak Oscar is beef tenderloin topped with crab meat, asparagus and Hollandaise sauce. It is a delicious recipe, but I think that my friend Oscar's version is a little more hip and definitely has more flavour.

1 lb.	asparagus	½ cup	chopped shallots
4	New York striploin steaks (each 8 oz.)	1 lb.	Dungeness crab meat, picked over
2 tbsp.	Great Canadian Steak Spice (page 97)	2 tbsp.	Dijon mustard
		2 tbsp.	whipping cream
½ cup	brandy	2 tsp.	chopped fresh dill
¼ cup	olive oil	2	green onions, finely chopped
4 cloves	garlic, minced		Cayenne pepper, black pepper and salt
¼ cup	butter	1	wheel Brie (125 g), cut into 12 wedges

1. Blanch asparagus in boiling water until tender-crisp. Cool under cold running water; drain. Cut into 1-inch pieces. Set aside.

2. Season steaks with the steak spice, pressing the seasoning into the meat. In a glass dish large enough to hold the steaks, whisk together the brandy, olive oil and garlic. Add steaks, turning to coat. Marinate, covered and refrigerated, for 1 to 2 hours.

3. Preheat grill to medium-high.

4. Melt the butter in a large frying pan over medium-high heat. Sauté the shallots for 2 to 3 minutes or until transparent and tender. Add asparagus; sauté for another 2 to 3 minutes. Add crab meat, mustard, whipping cream, dill and green onions. Bring to a boil. Remove from heat and season to taste with cayenne, black pepper and salt. Let cool slightly.

5. Remove steaks from marinade, reserving marinade. Grill for 3 to 4 minutes per side for medium-rare, basting with the marinade.

6. Divide crab mixture into 4 equal portions and spread 1 portion evenly on top of each steak. Top each steak with 3 slices of Brie. Close the lid and cook for 1 to 2 minutes or until the cheese starts to melt.

7. Serve immediately.

SERVES 4

Red-Rum Cowboy Steak

I remember my first cowboy steak. It was at Chef Mark Miller's Red Sage Restaurant in Washington, D.C., and it was truly amazing, weighing in at around 24 oz. Seasoned nicely with a BBQ rub and served with a mountain of crispy fried onions, Mark's steak is the benchmark for all other cowboy steaks.

2	bone-in rib steaks (each 24 oz. and 2 to 3 inches thick)	**RUM BUTTER SAUCE**	
½ cup	Red-Rum Rub (page 103)	6 tbsp.	cold butter (4 tbsp. cut into pieces)
		4 cloves	garlic, minced
		½ cup	dark rum
		¼ cup	BBQ sauce
			Salt to taste

1. Rub the steaks with the Red-Rum Rub. Marinate, covered and refrigerated, for 2 hours.

2. Preheat grill to medium-high.

3. Meanwhile, prepare the sauce. Melt 2 tbsp. of the butter in a small saucepan over medium-high heat. Add garlic; sauté for 2 to 3 minutes. Add rum. Bring to a boil and reduce liquid by half. Stir in BBQ sauce. Bring to a boil and remove from heat. Gradually whisk in the remaining butter until fully incorporated. Season with salt. Set aside.

4. Grill steaks for 8 to 12 minutes per side for medium-rare.

5. Slice each steak and serve drizzled with the sauce. You may have to fight over the bones.

SERVES 4

Spicy Marinated Sirloin Steak with Seafood Cream Sauce

I first did this recipe on the set of *Cottage Country* with a 4-lb. sirloin steak. The crew went crazy for the spicy tender grilled steak garnished with a rich shrimp cream sauce. This recipe, using 8-oz. individual sirloin steaks, is a little more user-friendly.

½ cup	orange juice	2 tbsp.	Hell's Fire Chili Paste (page 99)
¼ cup	soy sauce	4 cloves	garlic, chopped
¼ cup	olive oil	6	sirloin steaks (each 8 oz.)
			Seafood Cream Sauce (recipe follows)

1. In a glass dish large enough to hold the steaks, whisk together the orange juice, soy sauce and olive oil.

2. In a small bowl mix together the Hell's Fire Chili Paste and garlic. Wearing rubber gloves (as this mix may burn your hands), rub the steaks all over with the paste, pressing the seasoning into the meat. Place steaks in the orange juice mixture, turning to coat. Marinate, covered and refrigerated, for 4 to 6 hours.

3. Preheat grill to high.

4. Remove steaks from marinade and discard marinade. Grill the steaks for 4 to 5 minutes per side for medium-rare. Remove from the grill and let rest a few minutes before serving.

5. Thinly slice each steak and top with Seafood Cream Sauce.

SERVES 6

Seafood Cream Sauce

3 tbsp.	butter		1 cup	crab meat, picked over
4	shallots, finely chopped		1 cup	bay scallops
2 cloves	garlic, minced		2 tbsp.	brandy
3 tbsp.	all-purpose flour		1 tbsp.	chopped fresh parsley
1 tbsp.	Bone Dust BBQ Spice (page 97)		Dash	hot sauce
3 cups	chicken or fish stock		3	green onions, minced
1 cup	whipping cream			Salt and pepper to taste
1 cup	cooked baby shrimp			

1. In a medium saucepan over medium heat, melt the butter. Cook the shallots and garlic for 1 minute or until tender and translucent. Add the flour; cook, stirring, for 1 minute, being careful not to burn the flour. Stir in the BBQ spice.

2. Add the chicken stock a little at a time, whisking constantly to prevent lumps. Bring to a rolling boil, reduce heat and simmer for 30 minutes, stirring occasionally.

3. Stir in the cream and return to a boil.

4. Stir in the shrimp, crab, scallops, brandy, parsley, hot sauce, green onions, salt and pepper.

5. Serve immediately.

MAKES ABOUT 6 CUPS

The Big Man's Coffee-Crusted Porterhouse with Roquefort Butter

I dedicate this steak to me. I am a big man, and this is my steak.

4	porterhouse steaks (each 36 oz.)	½ cup	Mocha Coffee Rub (page 99)
			Olive oil
			Roquefort butter (recipe below)

1. Rub each steak with the Mocha Coffee Rub, pressing the seasoning into the meat. Brush steaks with olive oil and place in a glass dish. Marinate, covered and refrigerated, for 2 to 4 hours.

2. Preheat grill to high.

3. Grill the steaks for 10 to 12 minutes per side for medium.

4. Remove from the grill and let rest for 3 minutes.

5. Serve steaks topped with Roquefort Butter.

SERVES 4

Roquefort Butter

½ cup	unsalted butter, softened	2 tsp.	lemon juice
½ cup	crumbled Roquefort cheese	½ tsp.	Bone Dust BBQ Spice (page 97)
2 tsp.	chopped fresh rosemary		Salt to taste

1. In a food processor or mixing bowl, thoroughly blend the butter, Roquefort cheese, rosemary, lemon juice, BBQ spice and salt.

2. Transfer to a storage container and freeze until needed.

MAKES ABOUT 1 CUP

Rocketship 7 Peanut Butter and Jelly Steak

As a kid I used to spend some mornings watching Commander Tom on *Rocketship 7*, a kids' show out of Buffalo. It was pure silliness, and this recipe is a tribute to the show.

4	New York striploin steaks (each 12 oz.)	**PEPPERCORN PEANUT SAUCE**	
2 to		1 tbsp.	olive oil
3 tbsp.	Great Canadian Steak Spice (page 97)	1	large shallot, finely chopped
		¼ cup	sweet rice wine
	Cranberry Sauce (recipe follows)	⅓ cup	whipping cream
		¼ cup	smooth peanut butter
		2 tsp.	cracked black pepper
			Salt to taste

1. Season the steaks with the steak spice, pressing the seasoning into the meat. Marinate, covered and refrigerated, for 1 hour.

2. To prepare the sauce, heat the oil over medium-high heat in a medium saucepan. Add the shallots; sauté for 2 to 3 minutes or until tender. Add the sweet rice wine. Bring to a boil and reduce the liquid by half. Reduce heat to medium. Whisk in the cream and peanut butter until smooth. Stir in black pepper and salt. (If the sauce becomes too thick, just add a little water to thin it down.) Set aside and keep warm.

3. Preheat grill to high.

4. Grill steaks for 4 to 5 minutes per side for medium.

5. Thinly slice the steaks across the grain and drizzle with the peppercorn peanut sauce. Serve garnished with a tablespoon of Cranberry Sauce.

SERVES 4

Cranberry Sauce

1½ cups	cranberries (thawed if frozen), picked over	¼ cup	water
⅓ cup	sugar	¼ cup	orange juice

1. Wash and drain cranberries. Put berries, sugar, water and orange juice in a large saucepan. Slowly bring to a boil, stirring occasionally. Cover and cook, stirring occasionally, for 10 minutes or until the cranberries burst. Skim and cool.

MAKES ABOUT 1 CUP

GQ Magazine's Cedar-Planked Beef Tenderloin Stuffed with Blue Cheese

Beef and blue cheese are often found on the same table — think hefty steak with a forerunner of salad with blue cheese dressing. In this recipe I've gone one better by partnering these two full-flavoured items in one spectacular dish. So good even *GQ* wanted it!

6	well-aged beef tenderloin filets (each 6 oz.)	2 tbsp.	chopped fresh rosemary
		2 tbsp.	grainy mustard
6 tbsp.	blue cheese	2 tbsp.	olive oil
2 tsp.	fresh lemon juice	1 tbsp.	coarsely ground black pepper
	Salt and freshly ground black pepper to taste	1 tbsp.	balsamic vinegar
6 sprigs	fresh rosemary (about 8 inches long)	Special equipment: 1 untreated cedar plank	
6 cloves	garlic, minced	(10 x 8 x ⅝ inch), soaked in water overnight	

1. Using a sharp knife, make an incision 1-inch long in the side of each filet. Using your finger, make a pocket inside the filet. In a bowl, combine the blue cheese, lemon juice, salt and pepper. Mash together until well incorporated. Divide into 6 equal portions. Stuff into each filet, pushing the stuffing well into the centre. Wrap a sprig of rosemary around each stuffed filet. Secure with a toothpick.

2. In a glass dish, whisk together the garlic, chopped rosemary, mustard, oil, black pepper and vinegar. Place filets in the marinade, turning to coat completely. Marinate, covered and refrigerated, for 4 to 6 hours.

3. Preheat grill to high.

4. Place soaked cedar plank on the grill and close the lid. Bake the plank for 3 to 4 minutes or until it starts to crackle and smoke. Place the filets on the plank, evenly spaced. Close the lid and bake for 12 to 15 minutes for medium. Carefully open the lid (avoiding the billowing smoke) and remove filets from the grill.

5. Serve immediately.

SERVES 6

Grilled New York Strip Steak with Garlic Butter Escargots

I got this idea for steak and escargots from Chef Robert Clark of C Restaurant in Vancouver. His version is as delightful as mine. If you are ever in Vancouver be sure to eat at C. Robert's signature dish there is octopus bacon-wrapped scallops, a heavenly dish.

If your grill has a side burner, you can prepare the escargots while the steaks are grilling. If not, do step 4 before you grill the steaks and keep the escargots warm.

4	NY striploin steaks (each 12 oz.)	1	can (125 g) escargots, drained
2 tbsp.	Great Canadian Steak Spice (page 97)	¼ cup	cognac
		2 tbsp.	chopped fresh parsley
6 tbsp.	butter (4 tbsp. cut in pieces)	Pinch	nutmeg
8 cloves	garlic, minced		Salt and pepper
2	shallots, diced		

1. Preheat grill to medium-high.

2. Season the steaks with the steak spice, pressing the seasoning into the meat.

3. Grill the steaks for 3 to 4 minutes per side for medium-rare.

4. Meanwhile (or ahead of time), melt 2 tbsp. of the butter in a medium saucepan. Sauté the garlic and shallots for 2 to 3 minutes or until translucent and tender. Add the escargots; sauté for 3 to 4 minutes more until the snails are hot. Add the cognac and carefully flambé to remove the alcohol. When the flames have died down, stir in the remaining butter, parsley and nutmeg. Remove from heat and season to taste with salt and pepper.

5. Serve steaks topped with the garlic butter escargots.

SERVES 4

Roasted Red Pepper and Brie-Crusted Beef Tenderloin

I prepared this dish for the guests of Patrick Racing while at the CART Race in Chicago. I grilled 450 individual steaks for race day. Your recipe is for six, a little easier to prepare and just as delicious.

6	beef tenderloin filets (each 8 oz.)	4 cloves	garlic, minced
2 tbsp.	Great Canadian Steak Spice (page 97)	1 tbsp.	chopped fresh thyme
		2 tbsp.	balsamic vinegar
2	red bell peppers	2	green onions, chopped
2 tbsp.	olive oil	1	wheel Brie (125 g), diced
1	small yellow onion, sliced		Salt and pepper to taste

1. Preheat grill to medium-high.

2. Season the filets with the steak spice, pressing the seasoning into the meat. Marinate, covered and refrigerated, for 2 hours.

3. Roast peppers on the grill, turning periodically, until the peppers are charred and blistering. Place peppers in a plastic bag and seal tightly. (The heat from the peppers will produce steam that makes the skin easier to peel.) After 10 minutes peel and seed the peppers. Let cool.

4. Heat the oil in a frying pan over medium-high heat. Sauté the onion and garlic, stirring occasionally, for 5 to 10 minutes or until tender and slightly browned. Add the thyme and vinegar, stirring to scrape up any brown bits. Transfer to a bowl and let cool.

5. Preheat grill to medium-high.

6. Thinly slice or dice the roasted red peppers. Add to the onion and garlic. Add green onions, Brie, salt and pepper. Stir well. Shape into six ½-inch-thick patties about the same diameter as the filets.

7. Grill the filets for 3 to 4 minutes on one side. Turn steaks and top each with a pepper/Brie patty. Close the lid and cook for 3 to 4 more minutes for medium-rare.

8. Serve immediately.

SERVES 6

Teriyaki Steak

I like to add a little sambal chili paste to my teriyaki marinade to give it a little kick.

6	sirloin steaks (each 6 oz.)	¼ cup	rice wine vinegar
2 tbsp.	Indonesian Cinnamon Rub (page 100)	¼ cup	vegetable oil
		1 tbsp.	chopped fresh cilantro
TERIYAKI MARINADE		1 tbsp.	sesame oil
½ cup	dry sherry	2 tsp.	sambal chili paste
½ cup	soy sauce	1 tsp.	black pepper
⅓ cup	brown sugar	4	green onions, finely chopped
¼ cup	minced fresh ginger	4 cloves	garlic, minced

1. Season the steaks with the Indonesian Cinnamon Rub, pressing the seasoning into the meat. Place in a glass dish large enough to hold the steaks.

2. In a bowl combine the sherry, soy sauce, sugar, ginger, wine vinegar, vegetable oil, cilantro, sesame oil, sambal, pepper, green onions and garlic. Whisk until the sugar has dissolved. Reserve ½ cup of the teriyaki marinade for basting. Pour remaining marinade over steaks, turning to coat. Marinate, covered and refrigerated, for 4 hours.

3. Preheat grill to medium-high.

4. Remove steaks from marinade, discarding marinade. Grill steaks for 3 to 4 minutes per side for medium-rare, basting liberally with reserved teriyaki marinade.

5. Thinly slice each steak across the grain and serve.

SERVES 6

Grilled T-Bone Steak with Chimichurri Sauce

Chimichurri is an Argentinean sauce made with parsley, chilies and vinegar. It is full of flavour and is an excellent sauce for this big steak. Chimichurri also makes a great marinade.

4	T-bone steaks (each about 20 oz. and 1½ inches thick)	12 cloves	garlic
¼ cup	Bone Dust BBQ Spice (page 97)	2	jalapeño peppers, halved lengthwise
¼ cup	melted butter	½ cup	olive oil
		¼ cup	fresh oregano leaves
		¼ cup	red wine vinegar
CHIMICHURRI SAUCE		1 tbsp.	cracked black pepper
1 bunch	flat-leaf parsley	1 tsp.	ground cumin
6	green onions, cut into 2-inch lengths		Salt

1. Rub the steaks with the BBQ spice, pressing the seasoning into the meat. Marinate, covered and refrigerated, for 2 hours.

2. To make the sauce, in a food processor combine the parsley, green onions, garlic, jalapeño peppers, olive oil, oregano, vinegar, pepper and cumin. Pulse until coarsely blended. Season to taste with salt. Set aside.

3. Preheat grill to medium-high.

4. Grill steaks for 5 to 6 minutes per side for medium-rare, basting with melted butter during the final few minutes of grilling. Remove from grill and let steaks rest for 3 minutes.

5. Serve each steak drizzled with chimichurri sauce.

SERVES 4

Melanie's Steak Tartare

My dear friend and *Cottage Country* Chef Melanie Dunkelman created this wonderful recipe for steak tartare. I first tasted this dish when Mel worked for Chef Magyar Arpi at Splendido in Toronto. From that moment, I knew no one else could make it as well as Mel.

1 lb.	beef tenderloin, fully trimmed	1 tbsp.	ketchup
1	large shallot, finely diced	1 tbsp.	olive oil
½	jalapeño pepper, seeded and finely chopped	2 tsp.	Worcestershire sauce
			Salt and freshly ground black pepper to taste
2	egg yolks	Dash	hot sauce if you like it spicier (optional)
2 tbsp.	chopped flat-leaf parsley		A squeeze of lemon juice to increase the acidity
1 tbsp.	chopped capers		(optional)
1 tbsp.	Dijon mustard		

1. Using a sharp chef's knife, finely chop the beef tenderloin. Place in a large bowl.

2. Add the shallot, jalapeño pepper, egg yolks, parsley, capers, mustard, ketchup, olive oil, Worcestershire sauce, salt and pepper. Mix well with a wooden spoon. Adjust seasoning with hot sauce or lemon juice, if desired.

3. Divide the steak tartare among 4 plates. Serve with toasted thin slices of baguette and fries, if desired.

SERVES 4

Tip

When preparing this recipe, make sure your beef is very cold, because you do not want to serve warm steak tartare. Cold meat is also easier to chop. I prefer to use a chef's knife to chop the beef rather than a food processor, as the meat then has a better texture and looks more classical.

Raise a Little Hell Steaks

A tribute to one of my all-time favourite Canadian bar bands, Trooper. Fast, furious and fiery. This goes great with an ice-cold beer.

1	trimmed flank steak (2 lb.)	¼ cup	bourbon
½ cup	Hell's Fire Chili Paste (page 99)	¼ cup	olive oil

1. Using a sharp knife, score both sides of the flank steak in a diamond pattern making cuts ¼-inch deep. Rub the steak with the chili paste, pressing the paste into the meat.

2. In a glass dish large enough to hold the steak, whisk together the bourbon and olive oil. Add the steak, turning to coat. Marinate, covered and refrigerated, for 4 hours.

3. Preheat grill to medium-high.

4. Grill steak for 3 to 4 minutes for medium-rare. Remove from grill and let meat rest for 3 minutes.

5. Thinly slice the steak across the grain and serve with Grilled New Potato and Cheddar Salad (page 23), if desired.

SERVES 6

BBQ Beef Brisket

Smoked beef brisket is a Texas favourite, but it takes a long time to prepare over a low and slow grill. My version is a little quicker and provides tender, full-flavoured results.

1	beef brisket (5 lb.), trimmed	2 cups	chili sauce
¼ cup	Bone Dust BBQ Spice (page 97)	2 cups	BBQ sauce
6 cloves	garlic, minced	2 cans	ginger ale
1	large Spanish onion, sliced	2	bay leaves
3	jalapeño peppers, sliced		

1. Preheat oven to 350°F.

2. Season beef brisket with the BBQ spice, pressing the seasoning into the meat. Set aside.

3. In a large roasting pan toss together the garlic, onion and jalapeño peppers. Lay the brisket on top of the onion mixture.

4. In a bowl whisk together the chili sauce, BBQ sauce and ginger ale. Pour over brisket, making sure brisket is covered. (Make up more sauce if necessary.) Add the bay leaves. Cover tightly with lid or foil and cook for 2 to 2½ hours or until the meat is tender when pierced with a fork. Let cool slightly.

5. Preheat grill to medium-high.

6. Transfer brisket to a plate. Discard bay leaves. Transfer onion mixture to a saucepan and bring to a boil. Using a hand blender, purée the sauce. Adjust seasoning with salt and pepper.

7. Grill brisket for 15 to 20 minutes per side or until tender, basting liberally with sauce.

8. Thinly slice the brisket and serve with extra sauce and Memphis-Style Creamy Coleslaw (page 35), if desired.

SERVES 8

BBQ-Baked Cast-Iron-Pan Meat loaf

Meat loaf is not just for the oven anymore. Cooking meat loaf on a grill adds a wonderful smokiness to the meat. This recipe makes a hearty meat loaf.

1 lb.	ground chuck or sirloin		1 tbsp.	chopped garlic
1 lb.	regular ground pork		1 tbsp.	chopped fresh herbs
¾ cup	fresh bread crumbs		1 tbsp.	Bone Dust BBQ Spice (page 97)
¾ cup	BBQ sauce		1 tsp.	salt
2	eggs, lightly beaten		1½ cups	shredded aged Cheddar cheese
1	onion, diced			

Tip

Slice any leftovers 1-inch thick, grill them over low heat, basting with your favourite BBQ sauce, and serve on a fresh roll.

1. Preheat grill to high. Lightly grease a 10-inch cast-iron frying pan.

2. In a large bowl, thoroughly combine the ground chuck, ground pork, bread crumbs, BBQ sauce, eggs, onion, garlic, herbs, BBQ spice and salt. Turn the meat loaf mixture into the pan, pressing down firmly.

3. Place pan in grill, close the lid and bake for 35 to 50 minutes or until a meat thermometer reads 160°F. Top with the cheese and cook another 10 minutes or until the cheese melts.

4. Serve with BBQ Gravy (recipe follows) and Cheddar Mashed Potatoes with Grilled Onions (page 69), if desired.

SERVES 8

BBQ Gravy

¼ cup	butter	1½ cups	beef stock
2	onions, diced	1 cup	BBQ sauce
1 tsp.	chopped garlic		Salt and pepper to taste
¼ cup	all-purpose flour		

1. In a medium saucepan, melt the butter over medium heat. Sauté the onions and garlic for 2 to 3 minutes or until tender and transparent.

2. Add the flour and cook, stirring constantly, for 4 to 5 minutes, being careful not to burn the flour.

3. Add the beef stock ½ cup at a time, stirring constantly, until smooth and thickened.

4. Stir in the BBQ sauce, salt and pepper.

5. Reduce heat to low and simmer for 15 minutes, stirring occasionally. Strain and adjust seasoning.

MAKES 3 CUPS

Grilled Garlic Hanger Steak

Hanger steak is a relatively new steak on restaurant menus. It hangs between the rib cage and loin cage. Hanger steaks have a little stronger flavour than regular steaks and need to be very fresh. Ask your butcher for this tender and delicious piece of meat, as you will not find it in grocery stores.

1	hanger steak (1 lb.), trimmed	**Salt and pepper to taste**
2 tbsp.	Gilroy Roasted Garlic Paste (page 96)	

---

1. Rub the hanger steak all over with the roasted garlic paste. Marinate, covered and refrigerated, for 1 hour.

2. Preheat grill to high.

3. Season steak with salt and pepper. Grill for 5 to 6 minutes per side for medium-rare. Remove from grill and let rest for 3 or 4 minutes.

4. Thinly slice across the grain and serve with Dijon mustard and horseradish.

SERVES 2

Roll in the Hay Wrapped Steak #2 with Gentleman's Relish

Wrapping a steak in hay is one of my favourite ways to prepare a steak. Version #1 of this recipe appeared in my *Sticks and Stones Cookbook*. This is my second version.

4	rib-eye steaks (each 8 oz.)	1 bunch	rosemary, partially dried
½ cup	Herb Mustard Rub (page 100)	1 bunch	oregano, partially dried
¼ cup	olive oil	1 bunch	thyme, partially dried
4 handfuls	hay	1	bottle (750 mL) inexpensive red wine

1. Rub steaks with the Herb Mustard Rub, pressing the seasoning firmly into the meat. In a glass dish large enough to hold the steaks, whisk together the remaining wine and the olive oil. Add the steaks, turning to coat. Marinate, covered and refrigerated, for 1 hour.

2. In a large bucket soak the hay, rosemary, oregano and thyme in three-quarters of the wine for at least 30 minutes.

3. Preheat grill to high.

4. Remove a handful of hay from the wine and shake off excess liquid. On a work surface spread the hay evenly to approximately double the length of a steak. Place 1 steak at the bottom end of the hay. Carefully roll up the steak in the hay. Repeat with the remaining steaks.

5. Place wrapped steaks on the grill and close the lid. After 7 or 8 minutes carefully open the lid. Be careful — when you open the lid, the hay will be fed with oxygen and burn much faster. The hay will burn off and sear the meat. Turn the steaks and grill for another 3 to 4 minutes for medium-rare.

6. Serve each steak with a dollop of Gentleman's Relish (recipe follows).

SERVES 4

Gentleman's Relish

This is my version of the classic Harrods recipe.

½ cup	chopped shallots	1 tbsp.	chopped fresh parsley
½ cup	chopped green olives	1 tbsp.	chopped fresh thyme
¼ cup	coarsely chopped capers	6	anchovy fillets, finely chopped
¼ cup	coarsely chopped gherkins	2 cloves	garlic, chopped
¼ cup	olive oil	1 tsp.	cracked black pepper
2 tbsp.	grainy mustard		Salt to taste
2 tbsp.	lemon juice		

1. In a bowl combine the shallots, olives, capers, gherkins, olive oil, mustard, lemon juice, parsley, thyme, anchovies, garlic, pepper and salt (be careful adding salt as the capers and anchovies are quite salty).

2. Cover and refrigerate for 2 hours before using. Will keep for up to 2 weeks.

MAKES ABOUT 2 CUPS

Roberto Moreno's Lime Veal Chop

I was CART race car driver Roberto Moreno's chef for the 2000 race season, and one of his favourite dishes to eat after a race is a grilled veal chop marinated in fresh lime juice. A simple and delicious meal.

4	limes	¼ cup	olive oil
2 tbsp.	chopped fresh rosemary	4	bone-in veal rack chops (each 16 oz.)
2 tbsp.	Dijon mustard		Salt to taste
4 cloves	garlic, minced		

1. Cut 1 lime into 8 slices; set aside. Zest 1 lime and juice 3 limes.

2. In a glass dish large enough to hold the chops, whisk together the lime zest and juice, rosemary, mustard, garlic and olive oil. Add the chops, turning to coat. Marinate, covered and refrigerated, for 4 to 6 hours.

3. Preheat grill to medium-high.

4. Remove chops from marinade, reserving marinade. Season chops with salt. Grill for 6 to 8 minutes per side for medium-rare, basting with marinade.

5. Meanwhile, grill the lime slices until tender and lightly charred.

6. Serve each veal chop garnished with 2 grilled lime slices.

SERVES 4

Veal Tenderloin with Roasted Garlic, Gorgonzola and Mushrooms

Three of my all-time favourite foods served with succulent veal tenderloin. Who could ask for more?

2 heads	garlic	4	shallots, diced
2 tbsp.	olive oil	1 cup	sliced brown mushrooms
	Salt and freshly ground	1 cup	sliced shiitake mushrooms
	black pepper	1 cup	quartered chanterelle mushrooms
4	veal tenderloin filets (each 6 oz.	2 tbsp.	balsamic vinegar
	and 1½ inches thick)	1 tbsp.	chopped fresh thyme
¼ cup	Gilroy Roasted Garlic Paste (page 96)	¼ cup	veal stock
2 tbsp.	butter	1 cup	crumbled Gorgonzola cheese

1. Preheat oven to 325°F.

2. Peel papery outer skins from garlic. Cut the top third off each of the heads, exposing the cloves. Drizzle each with olive oil and season to taste with salt and pepper. Wrap in foil. Roast garlic for 45 to 60 minutes or until tender and golden brown. Open foil package and let garlic cool slightly. Squeeze roasted garlic into a small bowl and set aside.

3. Meanwhile, rub the filets with the roasted garlic paste, pressing the paste into the meat. Marinate, covered and refrigerated, for 30 minutes.

4. Preheat grill to medium-high.

5. Melt the butter in a frying pan over medium-high heat. Sauté the shallots for 2 minutes or until tender and translucent. Add all the mushrooms; sauté for 8 to 10 minutes, stirring, until tender. Stir in the vinegar, thyme and roasted garlic. Add the veal stock, bring to a boil and reduce liquid by half. Season to taste with salt and pepper and remove from heat. Set aside and keep warm.

6. Grill the veal for 3 to 4 minutes per side for medium-rare.

7. Toss the mushroom mixture with the Gorgonzola cheese and serve over each grilled tenderloin.

SERVES 4

Sour Mash Whiskey Grilled Pork Tenderloin

Lynchburg, Tennessee, is the home of Jack Daniel's Sour Mash Whiskey. For a refreshing summertime drink, add 6 oz. lemonade to 2 shots of whiskey and serve with a sprig of mint.

3	pork tenderloins (each ¾ to 1 lb.), trimmed	2 cups	brown sugar
½ cup	Licorice Rub (page 103)	¼ cup	Jack Daniel's Sour Mash Whiskey
		¼ cup	beef stock
		¼ cup	water
SOUR MASH WHISKEY GLAZING SAUCE		2 tbsp.	red wine vinegar
2 tbsp.	butter	2 tbsp.	Worcestershire sauce
4 cloves	garlic, minced	1 tbsp.	hot sauce
1	small onion, finely diced		Salt and pepper
1 tbsp.	chopped fresh sage		

1. Rub the tenderloins with the Licorice Rub, pressing the seasoning into the meat. Marinate, covered and refrigerated, for 4 hours.

2. In a medium saucepan melt the butter over medium-high heat. Sauté the garlic and onion for 3 to 4 minutes, stirring, until translucent and tender. Add the sage; cook, stirring, for 2 more minutes. Stir in the sugar, whiskey, stock, water, vinegar, Worcestershire sauce and hot sauce. Bring to a boil, reduce heat and simmer for 15 minutes, stirring occasionally. Season to taste with salt and pepper. Set aside.

3. Preheat grill to medium-high.

4. Grill tenderloins for 6 to 8 minutes per side for medium, basting liberally with whiskey sauce.

5. Remove tenderloins from grill and let rest for 5 minutes. Thinly slice and serve glazed with remaining sauce.

SERVES 6

Apple Cider Pork Butt Steaks

My friend Olaf loves pork shoulder butt steaks. He says it's the best part of the pig and provides the most flavour when marinated in apple cider and grilled. Serve these steaks with grilled apple slices and Ruby Red Cabbage Slaw (page 34).

1 cup	apple cider	1	onion, sliced
½ cup	honey	3	green onions, sliced
¼ cup	soy sauce	6	pork shoulder butt steaks
1 tbsp.	cracked black pepper		(each 8 oz. and 1½ inches thick)
1 tbsp.	chopped fresh cilantro		Salt to taste
8 cloves	garlic, chopped		

1. In a glass dish large enough to hold the steaks, stir together the cider, honey, soy sauce, pepper, cilantro, garlic, onion slices and green onions. Add the steaks, turning to coat. Marinate, covered and refrigerated, for 4 to 6 hours.

2. Preheat grill to medium-high.

3. Remove pork steaks from marinade and season with salt. Transfer marinade to a saucepan. Bring to a boil and reduce liquid by one-third. Using a hand blender, purée cider sauce until smooth.

4. Grill steaks for 5 to 6 minutes per side, basting liberally with cider sauce. Serve steaks drizzled with extra cider sauce.

SERVES 6

Beer Brine–Marinated Rotisserie of Pork Loin with Grilled Pineapple BBQ Sauce

Use a dark ale or strong lager to marinate the pork. It adds a nice nutty flavour.

1	boneless pork loin (4 lb. and 12 to 18 inches long)	½ cup	brown sugar
		¼ cup	salt
½ cup	Indonesian Cinnamon Rub (page 100)	6 cups	Grilled Pineapple BBQ Sauce (recipe follows)
4 bottles	dark beer		
1 cup	water		Special equipment: grill rotisserie rod

1. Rub the pork loin with the Indonesian seasoning, pressing the spices into the meat.

2. In a deep roasting pan or large plastic bag, whisk together the beer, water, brown sugar and salt. Add pork loin, turning to coat. Marinate, covered and refrigerated, for 24 hours.

3. Preheat grill to high.

4. Remove pork from marinade, discarding marinade. Skewer pork with the rotisserie rod. Secure with the rotisserie spikes.

5. Place pork on the grill. Season with salt, close the lid and sear pork for 15 minutes.

6. Reduce heat to medium-low and cook, basting frequently with Pineapple BBQ Sauce, for 1 to 1½ hours or until a meat thermometer reads 150°F for medium.

7. Remove pork from the rotisserie. Carefully remove rotisserie rod. Let meat rest for 10 minutes. Give a final baste and cut into 1-inch-thick slices.

8. Serve with extra pineapple sauce.

SERVES 8

Grilled Pineapple BBQ Sauce

1	pineapple, peeled and sliced into ½-inch-thick rounds	3 cloves	garlic, minced
		3 cups	hickory smoke–flavoured BBQ sauce
4 tbsp.	vegetable oil	½ cup	brown sugar
	Salt and pepper to taste	½ cup	bourbon
1	small onion, diced	¼ cup	Dijon mustard

1. Preheat grill to medium-high.

2. Rub 2 tbsp. of the vegetable oil all over the pineapple slices and season slices with salt and pepper.

3. Grill pineapple for 3 to 4 minutes per side or until golden brown, tender and lightly charred. Let cool. Cut pineapple into ¼-inch cubes.

4. In a large saucepan heat the remaining 2 tbsp. oil. Add the onion and garlic; sauté for 3 to 4 minutes or until tender. Add BBQ sauce, brown sugar, bourbon and mustard. Bring slowly to a boil, stirring.

5. Stir in pineapple. Adjust seasoning.

MAKES ABOUT 6 CUPS

Southern BBQ Pulled Pork

True Southern BBQ is slow roasted and smoked for hours over moderately hot coals. It takes some time, but the result is mouthwatering and absolutely fantastic. A charcoal grill will give you the best flavour, but you can also use a gas grill. Keep the temperature at medium-low and place your soaked wood chips in a metal smoking tray on the grill beside the meat.

Pulled, by the way, means shredded.

1	lemon, sliced	
1	large onion, sliced	
8 cloves	garlic, minced	
2 tbsp.	mustard seeds	
2 tbsp.	dried marjoram	
2 tbsp.	salt	
3 cans	Sprite	
1 cup	water	
1	pork shoulder roast (4 to 5 lb.)	
¼ cup	Bone Dust BBQ Spice (page 97)	
	Mesquite, hickory or cherry wood smoking chips, soaked in water for 30 minutes (optional)	

CAROLINA VINEGAR BBQ SAUCE

¾ cup	cider vinegar
¼ cup	brown sugar
1 cup	ketchup
1 tbsp.	Worcestershire sauce
1 tsp.	hot sauce
	Salt to taste

1. In a large pot combine the lemon, onion, garlic, mustard seeds, marjoram, salt, Sprite and water. Add the pork shoulder, turning to coat. Marinate, covered and refrigerated, for 24 to 48 hours.

2. Remove the pork shoulder from the marinade, discarding marinade. Rub with the BBQ spice, pressing the seasoning into the meat.

3. Prepare a charcoal grill for indirect cooking. Pile 3 to 4 lb. of charcoal on one side of the grill and set alight. Close the lid, leaving the vents at the bottom and top open. When the coals are grey and hot, place a foil pan of water on the grill over the hot coals. (This will add moisture to the dry heat of charcoal.) If desired, add soaked wood chips to the coals for the first 2 hours of cooking.

Continued ...

4. Place the pork shoulder on the grill opposite the hot coals. Close the lid and heat to 225 to 250°F. Adjust the vents at the base of the grill to maintain this temperature.

5. Cook pork for 5 to 6 hours or until a meat thermometer inserted into the thickest part of the meat reads 180°F and when you pull on the blade bone it pulls clean from the meat. Open the lid only to replenish the water and coals. If the meat looks dry, drizzle it with a little extra Sprite.

6. Remove the shoulder from the grill, cover with foil and let rest for 15 minutes.

7. Meanwhile, make the sauce. In a bowl whisk together the vinegar, sugar, ketchup, Worcestershire sauce, hot sauce and salt.

8. Remove the crackling skin from the pork and thinly slice. Pull the meat by hand or with a fork.

9. Place meat in a large bowl and add the sauce a little at a time, mixing thoroughly. Some like their pulled pork dry and others saucy.

10. Serve piled high on fresh buns alongside Ruby Red Cabbage Slaw (page 34), if desired.

SERVES 8

Sweet-and-Spicy Lamb Kebabs

Serve these grilled kebabs with grilled pita bread brushed with garlic and olive oil, and with grilled vegetable kebabs or salad.

1 cup	ketchup	1 tbsp.	crushed chilies
½ cup	steak sauce	1 tbsp.	coarsely ground black pepper
½ cup	honey	1 tsp.	hot sauce
¼ cup	malt vinegar	6 cloves	garlic, chopped
2 tbsp.	chopped fresh rosemary		Salt to taste
2 tbsp.	olive oil	1	boneless leg of lamb (3 lb.)

1. In a large bowl combine the ketchup, steak sauce, honey, vinegar, rosemary, oil, crushed chilies, pepper, hot sauce, garlic and salt. Set aside half of the mixture for basting.

2. Cut lamb into 1½-inch cubes. Add lamb to bowl, turning to coat. Marinate, covered and refrigerated, for 4 to 6 hours.

3. Preheat grill to medium-high. Soak 8 bamboo skewers in warm water for 30 minutes. (Or use metal skewers.)

4. Skewer 5 or 6 pieces of lamb onto each skewer. Discard marinade.

5. Grill the lamb skewers for 3 to 4 minutes per side for medium, basting frequently with reserved marinade.

SERVES 6 TO 8

Grilled Indian-Spiced Butterflied Leg of Lamb with Refreshing Raita

Inspired by the southwest flavours of India, here is a recipe for delicate lamb marinated with garam masala and served with a refreshing yogurt sauce. If you don't find garam masala in the spice section of your supermarket, look in the ethnic section of grocery stores and in Indian food shops.

1	boneless leg of lamb (4 to 5 lb.), butterflied	**RAITA**	
¼ cup +		1½ cups	plain yogurt
1 tsp.	garam masala	2 tbsp.	lime juice
10 cloves	garlic, minced	1 tbsp.	chopped fresh mint
1 cup	plain yogurt	2	plum tomatoes, seeded and chopped
½ cup	orange juice	1 clove	garlic, minced
2 tbsp.	olive oil	½	small red onion, diced
1 tbsp.	chopped fresh ginger	½	seedless cucumber, peeled and diced
1 tbsp.	chopped fresh mint		Salt to taste
2	red chilies, finely chopped		
4	green onions, chopped		
½ cup	clarified butter		

1. Rub the lamb with ¼ cup of the garam masala, pressing the spices into the meat.

2. In a glass dish large enough to hold the lamb, whisk together two-thirds of the garlic, the yogurt, orange juice, oil, ginger, mint, chilies and green onions. Add the lamb, turning to coat. Marinate, covered and refrigerated, for 4 to 6 hours.

3. To prepare the raita, in a bowl combine the yogurt, lime juice, mint, tomatoes, garlic, onion, cucumber and salt. Cover and refrigerate for 1 hour to allow flavours to develop.

4. Preheat grill to medium-high.

5. In a small bowl combine the clarified butter, remaining garlic and remaining 1 tsp. of garam masala for basting the lamb.

6. Remove lamb from the marinade, scraping off the excess marinade. Discard marinade. Season lamb with salt.

7. Sear the lamb for 5 to 6 minutes per side, brushing with the garlic butter mixture. Reduce heat to medium-low, close the lid and grill the lamb, turning once and brushing liberally with the garlic butter, for 20 to 30 minutes or until a meat thermometer inserted into the thickest part of the meat reads 140 to 145°F for medium-rare.

8. Remove lamb from grill and let rest for 5 minutes.

9. Thinly slice and serve with raita.

SERVES 8

Grilled Lamb Chops with Cumin Raisin Marmalade Sauce

I like to have my butcher cut my lamb chops at least 2 inches thick. This not only gives me more meat to enjoy but also lessens the chance of overcooking this tender meat.

12	lamb chops (about 2 inches thick)	**CUMIN RAISIN MARMALADE SAUCE**	
¼ cup	Gilroy Roasted Garlic Paste (page 96)	2 tbsp.	butter
		1 tbsp.	chopped fresh ginger
¼ cup	malt vinegar	1 tsp.	ground cumin
¼ cup	orange juice	¼ cup	Grand Marnier
¼ cup	olive oil	1 cup	orange marmalade
2 tbsp.	grainy mustard	½ cup	orange juice
		½ cup	golden raisins
		1 tbsp.	chopped fresh mint
			Salt and pepper to taste

1. Rub the lamb chops with the roasted garlic paste, pressing the seasoning into the meat.

2. In a shallow dish whisk together the vinegar, orange juice, olive oil and mustard. Add the lamb chops, turning to coat. Marinate, covered and refrigerated, for 4 hours.

3. To prepare the marmalade sauce, melt the butter in a medium saucepan over medium heat. Sauté the ginger for 2 to 3 minutes or until tender. Add cumin; sauté for 1 minute, stirring.

4. Deglaze pan with Grand Marnier, stirring well. Add marmalade and orange juice, stirring until smooth. Bring mixture to a boil, reduce heat and simmer for 15 minutes.

5. Stir in raisins, mint, salt and pepper. Remove from heat and keep warm.

6. Preheat grill to medium-high.

7. Remove chops from marinade, reserving marinade. Grill chops for 6 to 8 minutes per side for medium-rare, basting with marinade.

8. Serve 3 chops per person drizzled liberally with the raisin marmalade sauce.

SERVES 4

Grilled Lamb Leg Steaks with Goat Cheese and Green Olive Tapenade

Ask your butcher to prepare these delicious, inexpensive steaks. They can be bone-in or boneless. Have them cut at least 1½ inches thick.

12 cloves	garlic, minced		**GREEN OLIVE TAPENADE**	
½ cup	dry sherry		1 cup	pitted green olives
¼ cup	sherry vinegar		¼ cup	capers
¼ cup	olive oil		3 tbsp.	chopped fresh parsley
2 tbsp.	chopped fresh rosemary		1 tbsp.	chopped fresh thyme
2 tbsp.	Dijon mustard		1 tbsp.	anchovy paste
2 tsp.	coarsely ground black pepper		1 tbsp.	lemon juice
6	lamb leg steaks (each 8 oz. and 1½ inches thick)		4 cloves	garlic, chopped
			¼ cup	balsamic vinegar
			¼ cup	olive oil
				Salt and pepper to taste
			1 cup	crumbled goat cheese, softened

1. In a glass dish large enough to hold the steaks, whisk together the garlic, sherry, vinegar, oil, rosemary, mustard and pepper. Add lamb steaks, turning to coat. Marinate, covered and refrigerated, 4 to 6 hours.

2. Make the tapenade. In a food processor pulse the olives, capers, parsley, thyme, anchovy paste, lemon juice and garlic until coarsely chopped. Add vinegar and oil; pulse until incorporated. Season with salt and pepper. Transfer to a bowl and blend in goat cheese. Adjust seasoning. Refrigerate until needed.

3. Preheat grill to medium-high.

4. Remove lamb steaks from marinade, reserving marinade. Grill for 5 to 6 minutes per side for medium-rare, basting with marinade.

5. Serve each steak topped with a large dollop of the tapenade.

SERVES 6

Grilled Venison Rack with Blueberry Compote

In 1997 five chef friends and I had the pleasure of teaching for a few days at the Chef John Folse Culinary Institute in Thibodaux, Louisiana. We prepared a Canadian-themed six-course dinner for the alumni and invited guests. We flew in Canadian Red Deer venison, which I prepared on an enormous smoker/grill.

2 racks	frenched venison (4 bones each)		**BLUEBERRY COMPOTE**	
¼ cup	Malabar Pepper Rub (page 96)		2 cups	fresh or frozen blueberries
¼ cup	maple syrup		½ cup	sugar
¼ cup	grainy mustard		½ cup	water
¼ cup	Canadian whisky		¼ cup	Canadian whisky
¼ cup	olive oil		½ tsp.	vanilla
2 tbsp.	dried savory			
6 cloves	garlic, minced			
	Salt to taste			

1. Season the venison racks with the pepper rub, pressing the seasoning into the meat.

2. In a glass dish large enough to hold the racks, whisk together the maple syrup, mustard, whisky, oil, savory, garlic and salt. Add the racks, turning to coat. Marinate, covered and refrigerated, for 4 to 6 hours.

3. Preheat grill to medium-high.

4. To make the compote, in a medium saucepan combine the blueberries, sugar, water, whisky and vanilla. Bring to a boil, reduce heat and simmer, stirring occasionally, for 20 to 30 minutes or until the berries burst and the sauce is thickened. Set aside and keep warm.

5. Remove venison racks from marinade, reserving marinade. Grill racks for 7 to 8 minutes per side for medium-rare, basting with marinade. Remove racks from grill and let rest for 5 minutes.

6. Meanwhile, reheat blueberry compote if necessary.

7. Cut each rack into 4 thick chops and spoon blueberry compote over each chop.

SERVES 8

Grilled Buffalo Steaks with Apricot Cognac Sauce

Buffalo meat is a little more full flavoured than beef. Rare to medium-rare is the best way to serve tender and moist buffalo. If you overcook buffalo it will be dry and tough.

6	buffalo striploin steaks (each 6 to 8 oz.)	**APRICOT COGNAC SAUCE**	
2 tbsp.	Bone Dust BBQ Spice (page 97)	2 tbsp.	butter
1 cup	port wine	3	shallots, diced
½ cup	olive oil	6	dried apricots, chopped
2 tbsp.	Dijon mustard	¼ cup	white wine vinegar
1 tbsp.	chopped fresh rosemary	1 cup	chicken stock
1 tsp.	cracked black pepper	¼ cup	apricot jam
8	juniper berries	½ cup	cognac
4 cloves	garlic, minced		Salt and pepper

1. Season steaks with the BBQ spice, pressing the seasoning into the meat.

2. In a glass dish large enough to hold the steaks, whisk together the port, olive oil, mustard, rosemary, pepper, juniper berries and garlic. Add buffalo steaks, turning to coat. Marinate, covered and refrigerated, for 4 hours.

3. Meanwhile, prepare the sauce. In a small saucepan over medium-high heat, melt the butter. Sauté the shallots, stirring, for 2 minutes or until translucent and tender. Add the apricots; sauté for 1 minute more. Add the vinegar; bring to a boil and reduce liquid by half. Add the chicken stock and apricot jam. Return to a boil, reduce heat and simmer for 10 minutes.

4. Remove from heat. Using a hand blender, blend sauce until smooth. Return to heat, stir in cognac and bring to a boil. Season to taste with salt and pepper. Remove from heat and keep warm.

5. Preheat grill to medium-high.

6. Remove buffalo steaks from marinade, discarding marinade. Grill for 2 to 3 minutes per side for medium-rare.

7. Serve steaks topped with apricot cognac sauce.

SERVES 6

Breasts and Thighs

Chicken

Turkey

Cornish Hen

Quail

Butterflied Quail with Raspberry Syrup ... 190

Duck

Grilled Duck Breasts with Vanilla Rhubarb
    Chutney ... 191

Grilled Boneless Half-Chicken with Sweet-and-Sour BBQ Sauce

Years ago when I was a chef at Perry's Restaurant in Toronto I served this dish as a special every Thursday evening. There was one customer who would come in religiously every week and have two orders to himself.

Ask your butcher to debone the half-chickens, leaving the skin intact.

4	boneless skin-on half-chickens	2 tbsp.	chopped fresh rosemary
2 tbsp.	Bone Dust BBQ Spice (page 97)	2 tbsp.	olive oil
		1 tsp.	Worcestershire sauce
SWEET-AND-SOUR BBQ SAUCE		4 cloves	garlic, minced
1 cup	honey		Hot sauce to taste
½ cup	ketchup		Salt and pepper to taste
¼ cup	lemon juice		

1. Season the chicken with the BBQ spice. Marinate, covered and refrigerated, for 4 to 6 hours.

2. To prepare the sauce, in a small saucepan whisk together the honey, ketchup, lemon juice, rosemary, olive oil, Worcestershire sauce, garlic and hot sauce. Over medium heat, stirring occasionally, bring the sauce to a boil. Reduce heat to low and simmer for 10 minutes, stirring occasionally. Season with salt and pepper. Let cool.

3. Preheat grill to medium-high.

4. Grill the chicken skin side down for 6 to 8 minutes. Turn and baste the skin liberally with the sauce. Grill for another 6 to 8 minutes. Turn again and baste the meat side. Remove chicken from the grill.

5. Serve with the remaining sauce.

SERVES 4

Citrus Chicken Breasts with Papaya Salsa

The juices of lemon, lime and orange make a terrific marinade.

6	boneless skinless chicken breasts (each 6 oz.)	**PAPAYA SALSA**	
2 tbsp.	Indonesian Cinnamon Rub (page 100)	1	ripe papaya, peeled, seeded and diced
1	lemon, juiced	1	small red onion, diced
1	orange, juiced	1	red bell pepper, diced
2	limes, juiced	2	green onions, finely chopped
3 cloves	garlic, minced	1	jalapeño pepper, finely chopped
1	jalapeño pepper, finely chopped	2 tbsp.	lime juice
1 tbsp.	chopped fresh ginger	1 tbsp.	chopped fresh cilantro
1 tbsp.	chopped fresh cilantro	1 tbsp.	olive oil
	Salt to taste	2 tsp.	chopped fresh mint
			Salt and freshly ground black pepper to taste

1. Rub the chicken with the Indonesian rub, pressing the seasoning into the meat.

2. In a glass dish, whisk together the lemon juice, orange juice, lime juice, garlic, jalapeño pepper, ginger and cilantro. Add chicken breasts, turning to coat. Marinate, covered and refrigerated, for 4 to 6 hours.

3. Meanwhile, prepare the papaya salsa. In a bowl combine the papaya, red onion, red pepper, green onions, jalapeño pepper, lime juice, cilantro, oil, mint, salt and pepper.

4. Preheat grill to medium-high.

5. Remove chicken breasts from marinade, discarding marinade, and season with salt. Grill for 5 to 6 minutes per side or until golden brown and fully cooked.

6. Top each chicken breast with a spoonful of papaya salsa and serve.

SERVES 6

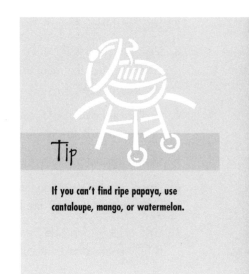

Tip

If you can't find ripe papaya, use cantaloupe, mango, or watermelon.

Grilled Chicken Breasts Stuffed with Goat Cheese and Prosciutto

Rich goat cheese blended with Italian prosciutto makes a delicious stuffing for chicken. My friend Rosa's mother first made a version of this chicken for me to try. I've since modified it for the grill. Rosa, it's fantastic!

8	boneless skin-on chicken breasts (each 6 oz.)	½ cup	crumbled goat cheese
¼ cup	Bone Dust BBQ Spice (page 97)	½ cup	finely chopped dried apricots
	Salt and pepper to taste	1 tbsp.	chopped fresh oregano
1 cup	julienned prosciutto	1 tbsp.	balsamic vinegar
1 cup	ricotta cheese	1 tsp.	coarsely ground black pepper
		2	green onions, finely chopped

1. Preheat grill to medium-high.

2. Lay the chicken breasts skin side down. Remove the chicken tenderloins. Lightly pound the tenderloins flat. Set aside.

3. Using a sharp knife, cut a pocket about 1-inch deep from the top of the breast to the bottom. Using your fingers, carefully push the meat aside to make a large pocket. Season the chicken inside and out with the BBQ spice, salt and pepper.

4. In a large bowl mix together the prosciutto, ricotta, goat cheese, apricots, oregano, vinegar, pepper and green onions. Season to taste with salt.

5. Divide the stuffing into 8 equal portions and shape each portion into a firmly packed oval.

6. Place 1 stuffing portion into each chicken cavity. Place a flattened tenderloin over the cavity and tuck the tenderloin into the opening, firmly pressing the edges to make a tight seal.

7. Grill chicken skin side down for 6 to 8 minutes, then turn and grill for another 6 to 8 minutes or until the chicken is fully cooked and the stuffing is hot.

SERVES 8

Honey Mustard Chicken Thighs

Chicken thighs are already the tastiest part of the bird. Add this sauce and you'll have an instant BBQ favourite.

8 cloves	garlic, minced	1 tbsp.	finely chopped fresh ginger
¼ cup	honey	1 tbsp.	chopped fresh cilantro
¼ cup	prepared mustard	2 tsp.	lemon pepper
2 tbsp.	soy sauce	12	chicken thighs
2 tbsp.	lemon juice		Salt to taste

1. In a medium bowl combine the garlic, honey, mustard, soy sauce, lemon juice, ginger, cilantro and lemon pepper.

2. Place chicken thighs in a glass dish and pour half of the honey mustard mixture over the chicken, turning to coat. Marinate, covered and refrigerated, for 4 hours. Reserve the remaining sauce for basting.

3. Preheat grill to medium-high.

4. Remove thighs from marinade, discarding marinade, and grill for 6 to 8 minutes per side, basting liberally during the final 5 minutes of grilling with reserved honey mustard sauce.

5. Serve immediately with Singapore Noodle Salad (page 34), if desired.

SERVES 6

Orange Teriyaki Chicken Thighs

Big flavours from the grill are made easy with flavourful chicken thighs and a sweet teriyaki sauce.

12	boneless chicken thighs	⅓ cup	corn syrup
1 tbsp.	Bone Dust BBQ Spice (page 97)	¼ cup	minced fresh ginger
		¼ cup	vegetable oil
ORANGE TERIYAKI MARINADE		¼ cup	rice wine vinegar
4	green onions, finely chopped	1 tbsp.	chopped fresh cilantro
4 cloves	garlic, minced	1 tbsp.	sesame oil
½ cup	orange juice	2 tsp.	sesame seeds
½ cup	soy sauce	1 tsp.	coarsely ground black pepper

Tip

For a little zing add some freshly grated horseradish!

1. Soak twenty-four 6-inch bamboo skewers in warm water for 1 hour.

2. Rub the chicken with the BBQ spice, pressing the seasoning into the meat. Skewer each thigh with 2 skewers. (This will help keep the chicken flat on the grill.) Place thighs in a glass dish.

3. In a bowl whisk together the green onions, garlic, orange juice, soy sauce, corn syrup, ginger, vegetable oil, vinegar, cilantro, sesame oil, sesame seeds and black pepper. Pour half of the mixture over the chicken, turning to coat. Marinate, covered and refrigerated, for 4 to 6 hours. Reserve the remaining marinade for basting.

4. Preheat grill to medium-high.

5. Remove chicken thighs from marinade, discarding marinade, and grill for 4 to 5 minutes per side or until fully cooked and slightly charred, basting frequently with reserved marinade.

SERVES 6

Maple Garlic Chicken Drumsticks

Grilled chicken drumsticks are a perfect accompaniment to any summer picnic. These can be served hot or prepared ahead and served cold.

4 cloves	garlic, minced		1 tsp.	sesame seeds
2	green onions, minced		1 tsp.	sesame oil
1	jalapeño pepper, finely chopped		12	chicken drumsticks
¼ cup	Dijon mustard			Salt and freshly ground black pepper to taste
¼ cup	maple syrup			

1. Preheat grill to medium-high.

2. In a large bowl whisk together the garlic, green onions, jalapeño pepper, mustard, maple syrup, sesame seeds and sesame oil.

3. Season the chicken with salt and pepper. Place chicken in a grill basket.

4. Grill chicken for 8 to 10 minutes per side or until fully cooked, basting liberally with the maple mixture.

5. Carefully remove chicken from grill basket and toss in remaining maple mixture.

6. Serve immediately or cool thoroughly and place in an airtight container for a picnic.

SERVES 6

Tip

If you do not have maple syrup, substitute corn syrup or honey.

Devil's Brewed Roast Chicken with White Trash BBQ Sauce

This fun and tasty recipe is a version of classic Texas Drunken Chicken. I first learned of this wonderful way of cooking chicken while on a visit to the Kansas City BBQ Competition. It makes a moist and tender chicken with a crispy outside.

    While at the Grand Prix of Houston I prepared this recipe for the pit crew. I grill-roasted 32 drunken chickens at once on our massive grill. It was a sight to behold — and what an aroma!

2	chickens (each 3–4 lb.)	¼ cup	hot sauce
½ cup	Bone Dust BBQ Spice (page 97)	2 tbsp.	lemon juice
2	cans (each 375 mL) lager or ale		
¼ cup	butter		**Special equipment: 4 foil pie plates**

1. Preheat grill to medium-high.

2. Wash the chickens inside and out with cold water and pat dry with paper towels. Rub the chickens inside and out with the BBQ spice, pushing the rub firmly onto the birds so it adheres.

3. Open the beer cans. Take a sip out of each beer for good luck. Just a sip, now — not the whole can.

4. Put 1 pie plate inside another. Place 1 beer can on the doubled-up pie plates. Place 1 chicken over the beer can so that the beer can is in the cavity of the bird and the bird is standing upright. Repeat for the other chicken.

5. To prepare the basting sauce, in a small saucepan over medium heat, melt the butter. Stir in the hot sauce and lemon juice. Heat, stirring, until mixed.

6. Place the chickens on their pie plates on the grill. Close the lid and roast the chickens for 50 to 60 minutes or until fully cooked and golden brown, basting liberally with the sauce. (To check for doneness insert a meat thermometer into the thigh. It should read 160°F.)

7. Serve with White Trash BBQ Sauce (recipe follows) and the juices that have collected in the pie plates.

SERVES 4 TO 6

White Trash BBQ Sauce

1 cup	ranch-style dressing		1 tbsp.	chopped fresh thyme
1 cup	mayonnaise		1 tbsp.	cracked black pepper
½ cup	whipping cream		1 tbsp.	Worcestershire sauce
½ cup	milk		2 tsp.	hot sauce
2 tbsp.	lemon juice		1 tsp.	salt
1 tbsp.	chopped fresh parsley		3 cloves	garlic, minced

1. In a medium saucepan combine all the ingredients. Over medium heat bring the mixture to a boil, stirring constantly. Adjust seasoning. Keep warm over low heat.

MAKES ABOUT 3½ CUPS

BBQ Jerk Turkey with Grilled Banana BBQ Sauce

On a recent trip to Jamaica I had the pleasure of eating jerk turkey with grilled bananas. In my version of this island dish, I make a sauce with the grilled bananas.

2	boneless skin-on turkey breasts (2 lb. total)	**GRILLED BANANA BBQ SAUCE**	
¼ cup	Jamaican Jerk Paste (page 109)	4	bananas, unpeeled
		2 tbsp.	vegetable oil
2 tbsp.	lime juice	1	onion, diced
2 tbsp.	vegetable oil	1 cup	gourmet BBQ sauce
		1 cup	chicken stock
		½ cup	orange juice
		1 tbsp.	Jamaican Jerk Paste (page 101)
		1 tbsp.	brown sugar
		1 tbsp.	cider vinegar

1. Wash and pat dry the turkey breasts. Mix together the jerk paste, lime juice and oil. Carefully push the jerk marinade under the skin and rub into the turkey meat and over the skin. Place in a glass dish and marinate, covered and refrigerated, for 4 to 6 hours.

2. Preheat grill to high.

3. To make the sauce, grill the unpeeled bananas until charred and tender. Peel the bananas.

4. In a medium saucepan over medium heat, heat the oil. Sauté the onion for 3 minutes or until tender. Add the bananas, BBQ sauce, chicken stock, orange juice, jerk paste, brown sugar and vinegar. Bring to a boil, reduce heat and simmer for 10 minutes, stirring occasionally.

5. In a blender or food processor, purée the sauce until smooth. Strain and cool.

6. Preheat grill to medium-high.

7. Grill the turkey breasts skin side down for 10 to 12 minutes. Turn and grill for another 10 to 12 minutes, basting liberally with the banana sauce. (The turkey is done when a meat thermometer reads 160°F.)

8. Thinly slice the turkey breasts and serve with remaining sauce.

SERVES 8 TO 12

Pineapple-Brined Smoked Turkey with Bourbon BBQ Sauce

There are no rules that say you can only eat turkey at Thanksgiving, Christmas or Easter. Roasting a turkey the traditional way with a savoury stuffing is outstanding, but when it comes to summertime, I like to smoke a turkey and baste it with a bourbon BBQ sauce.

1 bunch	savory, chopped		¼ cup	vegetable oil
10 cloves	garlic, smashed		¼ cup	Bone Dust BBQ Spice (page 97)
10	juniper berries			Hickory smoking chips soaked in water for 1 hour
4	bay leaves			
8 cups	pineapple juice		**BOURBON BBQ SAUCE**	
2 cups	sugar		2 cups	gourmet BBQ sauce
1 cup	salt		1 cup	pineapple juice
1	turkey (10–12 lb.)		½ cup	bourbon

1. In a large pot combine the savory, garlic, juniper berries, bay leaves, pineapple juice, sugar and salt. Bring to a boil, stirring occasionally. Remove from heat and cool completely.

2. Place the turkey in a bucket or other container large enough to hold it. Pour the pineapple brine over the turkey. Marinate, covered and refrigerated, for 24 hours.

3. Preheat grill to medium.

4. To make the sauce, combine the BBQ sauce, pineapple juice and bourbon.

5. Remove turkey from brine, discarding brine, and pat dry with paper towels. Rub turkey all over with the vegetable oil and then the BBQ spice. Place turkey in a large foil roasting pan. Tuck the legs and wings in close to the body.

6. Place the turkey on the grill, add smoking chips to coals or smoking box, close the lid and cook for 30 to 40 minutes per pound or until fully cooked, basting every 30 minutes with Bourbon BBQ Sauce and replenishing smoking chips as needed. (If the skin or wing tips should start to get black, cover the turkey with pieces of foil.) The turkey is cooked when a meat thermometer inserted in the thickest part of the thigh reads 180°F.

7. Let turkey rest for 15 minutes before carving.

SERVES 6 TO 10

Asian Grilled Turkey Steaks

Ask your butcher to prepare turkey steaks cut from the breast. Each steak should be at least 1-inch thick and weigh about 6 ounces.

4	green onions, thinly sliced	1 tbsp.	sesame oil
3 cloves	garlic, chopped	1 tsp.	sesame seeds
¼ cup	soy sauce	1 tsp.	crushed chilies
¼ cup	dry sherry		Salt and freshly ground black pepper to taste
2 tbsp.	maple syrup	6	turkey steaks (each 6 oz.)
1 tbsp.	chopped fresh ginger	½ cup	hoisin sauce
1 tbsp.	chopped fresh cilantro		

1. In a glass dish large enough to hold the turkey steaks, whisk together the green onions, garlic, soy sauce, sherry, maple syrup, ginger, cilantro, sesame oil, sesame seeds, crushed chilies, salt and pepper. Add the turkey, turning to coat. Marinate, covered and refrigerated, for 4 hours.

2. Preheat grill to medium-high.

3. Remove turkey steaks from marinade, discarding marinade, and grill for 4 to 5 minutes per side, basting liberally with hoisin sauce.

SERVES 6

Grand Marnier Cornish Hens

When preparing this recipe I always like to have a little extra Grand Marnier by the grill — for guzzling purposes.

4	Cornish game hens	1 tbsp.	mustard seeds
2	oranges, thinly sliced	1 tbsp.	cracked black pepper
1	onion, thinly sliced	½ cup	Grand Marnier
¼ cup	olive oil	¼ cup	melted butter
2 tbsp.	chopped fresh tarragon		Salt to taste
1 tbsp.	chopped fresh ginger		

1. Using poultry shears, split each Cornish hen down the middle on each side of the backbone to remove the backbone. Using a sharp knife, carefully debone the breast and legs.

2. In a glass dish large enough to hold the hens, combine the oranges, onion, olive oil, tarragon, ginger, mustard seeds, pepper and ¼ cup of the Grand Marnier. Add the hens, turning to coat. Marinate, covered and refrigerated, for 4 to 6 hours.

3. Preheat grill to medium-high.

4. Mix together the remaining ¼ cup of Grand Marnier and melted butter.

5. Remove hens from the marinade, discarding marinade, and season with salt. Grill hens skin side down for 5 to 6 minutes, basting with Grand Marnier butter. Turn and grill, basting, for another 5 to 6 minutes or until fully cooked, crisp and delicious.

SERVES 4

Butterflied Quail with Raspberry Syrup

Ask your butcher to butterfly and remove the backbone of the quail. Quails are small. One is fine as an appetizer but allow 2 or 3 per person for a main course.

RASPBERRY SYRUP

½ pint	raspberries
½ cup	brown sugar
½ cup	maple syrup
½ cup	water
¼ cup	Chambord or other raspberry liqueur

¼ cup	olive oil
¼ cup	raspberry vinegar
1 tbsp.	chopped fresh tarragon
12	quails, butterflied
	Salt and pepper to taste

---

1. To make the syrup, in a small saucepan combine the raspberries, brown sugar, maple syrup, water and Chambord. Bring to a boil, stirring, reduce heat to low and simmer for 10 minutes. Purée mixture in a blender. Strain through a fine sieve to remove seeds. Set aside.

2. In a large bowl whisk together the olive oil, raspberry vinegar and tarragon. Add quails, turning to coat. Marinate, refrigerated, for 1 to 2 hours.

3. Preheat grill to medium-high.

4. Remove quails from marinade, discarding marinade, and season with salt and pepper. Grill quails for 2 to 3 minutes per side, basting with the raspberry syrup.

5. Serve immediately with remaining raspberry syrup.

SERVES 6

Grilled Duck Breasts with Vanilla Rhubarb Chutney

Duck is best served rare or medium-rare. Be careful not to overcook it, or it will be tough.

4	boneless duck breasts (each 8–12 oz.)	3 stalks	rhubarb
		1	vanilla bean, split lengthwise
2 tbsp.	Malabar Pepper Rub (page 96)	¼ cup	sugar
		¼ cup	honey
VANILLA RHUBARB CHUTNEY		¼ cup	cider vinegar
2 tbsp.	olive oil	Pinch	ground mace
1	small red onion, diced	Pinch	ground allspice
1 tbsp.	chopped fresh ginger	¼ cup	Stoli brand vanilla-infused vodka

1. Using a sharp knife, score the skin side of the duck breasts in a diamond pattern, slicing about ¼-inch deep into the fat. Season the duck breasts with the Malabar pepper rub, pressing the seasoning into the meat. Set aside.

2. Preheat grill to medium-high.

3. To prepare the chutney, in a medium frying pan, heat the oil over medium-high heat until hot but not smoking. Add the onion and ginger; sauté for 2 to 3 minutes, stirring occasionally, until tender. Add the rhubarb and cook, stirring, until the rhubarb is a bit browned.

4. Add the vanilla bean, sugar, honey, vinegar, mace and allspice. Bring to a boil, stirring. Reduce heat to low and simmer for 10 minutes, stirring occasionally. Add the vodka and cook, stirring occasionally, for 5 more minutes. Set aside.

5. Grill the duck breasts skin side down for 4 to 6 minutes or until the skin is golden brown and crisp. (Be careful of flare-ups from the dripping duck fat. If flare-ups occur, reduce grill heat and move the duck breasts so they are not directly over the flames.) Turn the duck breasts and grill for another 5 to 8 minutes for medium-rare. The duck breasts should be golden brown and firm to the touch.

6. Thinly slice each breast and serve with Vanilla Rhubarb Chutney.

SERVES 4 TO 6

Wet 'n' Wild

Fish

Shellfish

Grilled Atlantic Salmon Fillets with Grapefruit Maple Mustard Glaze

Fresh grapefruit is a wonderful way to spark up any grilled seafood. Cut a grapefruit in half and squeeze the juice over the salmon just before serving to add a burst of flavour.

MARINADE AND GLAZE			
1 cup	ruby red grapefruit juice	8	Atlantic salmon fillets (each 6 oz.), skinned
½ cup	pure Canadian maple syrup	¼ cup	Salmon Seasoning (page 98)
2 tbsp.	chopped fresh dill	1½	grapefruits
2 tbsp.	whole-grain Dijon mustard		
2 tbsp.	olive oil		
1 tbsp.	coarsely ground black pepper		

1. In a small bowl whisk together the grapefruit juice, maple syrup, dill, mustard, olive oil and pepper.

2. Season the salmon with the salmon seasoning, pressing the seasoning into the flesh. Place the salmon evenly in a shallow dish large enough to hold it in one layer. Pour half of the marinade over the salmon, turning to coat. Marinate for 30 minutes, turning occasionally.

3. Place the remaining marinade in a small saucepan and warm it over medium heat.

4. Slice the whole grapefruit into ½-inch-thick slices. Set aside.

5. Preheat grill to medium-high.

6. Remove salmon from marinade, reserving marinade. On a lightly seasoned grill, grill the salmon for 3 to 4 minutes per side or until just cooked, basting with the marinade that you used to marinate the salmon.

7. While salmon is grilling, brush grapefruit slices with a little oil and grill for 2 to 3 minutes per side.

8. When the salmon is cooked, squeeze the ½ grapefruit over the fish.

9. Serve with grilled grapefruit slices and heated marinade.

SERVES 8

Apple Cider BBQ Atlantic Salmon

Salmon is my favourite fish. It is not only full of flavour but it's also very good for you — it's loaded with a healthy fat called the Omega-3 fatty acid.

APPLE CIDER BBQ SAUCE

2 tbsp.	olive oil
3 cloves	garlic, minced
3	shallots, finely chopped
1 cup	apple cider
1 cup	gourmet BBQ sauce

1 tbsp.	chopped fresh herbs (thyme, rosemary, sage)
1 tbsp.	fresh lemon juice
1 tsp.	coarsely ground black pepper
	Salt
6	Atlantic salmon fillets (each 6 oz.), skinned
1 to 2 tbsp.	Salmon Seasoning (page 98)

---

1. In a medium saucepan heat the olive oil over medium-high heat. Sauté the garlic and shallots for 2 to 3 minutes or until tender.

2. Add the apple cider; bring to a boil and reduce liquid by half. Add the BBQ sauce, herbs, lemon juice and black pepper. Return to a boil, reduce heat to low and simmer for 10 minutes. Season to taste with salt. Let cool slightly.

3. Preheat grill to medium-high.

4. Season the salmon with the salmon seasoning, pressing the seasoning into the flesh.

5. Grill the salmon for 4 to 5 minutes per side, basting liberally with the cider sauce.

6. Serve the salmon with an extra drizzling of sauce.

SERVES 6

Tandoori Planked Salmon

The flavour of tandoori seasoning and cedar work well together in this India-meets-the-Pacific-Northwest dish.

6	**Atlantic salmon fillets (each 6 oz.)**	**Special equipment: 1 untreated cedar plank**
	Tandoori Marinade (page 123)	**(at least 10 x 8 x 1 inch), soaked in water overnight**

1. Place the salmon in a large glass dish and pour the Tandoori Marinade over it, turning to coat. Marinate, covered and refrigerated, for 2 hours.

2. Preheat grill to high.

3. Place soaked plank on the grill and close the lid. Let the plank heat for 3 to 4 minutes or until it starts to crackle and smoke.

4. Remove salmon from marinade, scraping off excess marinade. Discard marinade.

5. Carefully open the lid and place the salmon on the plank. Close the lid and bake the salmon for 12 to 15 minutes or until it flakes easily with a fork. Periodically check the plank; if it is burning, spray it with water and reduce heat to medium.

6. Carefully remove the plank from the grill and serve the salmon immediately.

SERVES 6

Cedar-Planked Salmon with Citrus BBQ Sauce

Planking is one of the easiest ways to prepare seafood on the grill. It brings full flavour to salmon and other seafood without too much fuss.

CITRUS BBQ SAUCE				
1	small red onion, diced		2 tbsp.	orange juice
2 cloves	garlic, minced		1 tbsp.	coarsely ground black pepper
3	green onions, chopped			Salt to taste
1½ cups	BBQ sauce		6	Atlantic salmon fillets (each 6 oz.)
½ cup	orange marmalade			
¼ cup	chopped fresh dill		Special equipment: 1 untreated cedar plank (at least 10 x 8 x 1 inch), soaked in water overnight	

1. Preheat grill to high.

2. In a bowl combine the onion, garlic, green onions, BBQ sauce, marmalade, dill, orange juice, black pepper and salt. Heavily crust the top of each salmon fillet with the mixture, pressing down gently.

3. Place soaked plank on the grill and close the lid. Let the plank heat for 3 to 4 minutes or until it starts to crackle and smoke.

4. Carefully open the lid and place the salmon on the plank. Close the lid and bake the salmon for 12 to 15 minutes or until it flakes easily with a fork. Periodically check the plank; if it is burning, spray it with water and reduce heat to medium.

5. Carefully remove the plank from the grill and serve the salmon immediately.

SERVES 6

Cedar-Planked Haddock Stuffed with Crab, Shrimp and Cheddar Cheese

Planking is such an easy way to prepare seafood. You can almost stick it on the grill and forget it.

6	skinless haddock fillets (each 6 oz.)		½ cup	dry bread crumbs
	Salt and freshly ground black pepper to taste		¼ cup	melted butter
			1 tbsp.	chopped fresh dill
			1 tbsp.	lemon juice
1 cup	crab meat		2	shallots, finely chopped
1 cup	baby shrimp, roughly chopped		3	green onions, finely chopped
1 cup	shredded Cheddar cheese		1 clove	garlic, finely chopped

1. Preheat grill to high.

2. With a sharp knife, cut an incision lengthwise in the top of each fillet, cutting about three-quarters of the way through the fish. Using your fingers, open the incision to make a large pocket. Season the fillets with salt and pepper.

3. In a bowl combine the crab meat, shrimp, Cheddar cheese, bread crumbs, melted butter, dill, lemon juice, shallots, green onions and garlic. Season to taste with salt and freshly ground black pepper and mix thoroughly.

4. Divide the stuffing into 6 equal portions. Pack the stuffing into each of the pockets. It does not matter if some stuffing is on top of the fish.

5. Place soaked plank on the grill and close the lid. Let the plank heat for 3 to 4 minutes or until it starts to crackle and smoke.

6. Carefully open the lid and place the stuffed fillets on the plank. Close the lid and bake the haddock for 12 to 15 minutes or until it flakes easily with a fork. Periodically check the plank; if it is burning, spray it with water and reduce heat to medium.

7. Carefully remove the plank from the grill and serve the haddock with Creamed Spinach (page 64), if desired.

SERVES 6

Grilled Stuffed Arctic Char with Apricot Glaze

This recipe takes a bit of time to prepare, but it is easy to grill and dazzling on the plate.

2	leeks, trimmed, leaves separated and washed (16 leaves needed)		Salt and pepper to taste
¼ cup	butter	4	Arctic char (each about 1 lb.) or 8 fillets with skin
1	sweet onion, thinly sliced		**APRICOT GLAZE**
4 cloves	garlic, chopped	½ cup	apricot jam
2 tbsp.	chopped fresh sage	¼ cup	butter
½ cup	diced dried apricots	¼ cup	tangerine juice
1 tbsp.	lemon juice	1 tsp.	cracked black pepper

1. In a pot of boiling water, blanch the leek leaves for 1 minute or until tender and bright. Cool in ice water. Drain on paper towels.

2. In a medium frying pan over medium-high heat, melt the butter. Sauté the onion, garlic and sage for 3 minutes or until tender. Remove from heat and stir in the dried apricots, lemon juice, salt and pepper. Set aside.

3. If using whole fish, rinse the fish with cold water inside and out. Pat dry with paper towels. Fillet the fish, removing the head, backbone and rib cage. Season the fish with salt and pepper.

4. Lay 3 or 4 leek leaves on a work surface with the root ends facing you. Place 1 fillet skin side down crosswise across the leeks. Top evenly with one-quarter of the onion mixture. Lay a second fillet skin side up on the onion stuffing. Roll up the fish in the leeks to make a tight wrap. Repeat with other fish. Wrap tightly in plastic and refrigerate for 1 hour to allow the fish and leeks to set.

5. Preheat grill to medium-high.

6. To make the glaze, in a small saucepan combine the apricot jam, butter, tangerine juice and pepper. Heat, stirring, until melted and blended.

7. Unwrap fish from plastic and grill for 8 to 10 minutes per side, basting liberally with the glaze. Use a large spatula to turn the fish.

8. Slice the fish into 4 to 6 rounds and serve with a drizzling of apricot glaze.

SERVES 8

Grilled Sea Bass Fillets

Some chefs may like to serve sea bass rare to medium-rare, but I find it tastes better when just cooked through. It is then flaky and tender with lots of flavour.

1 tbsp.	olive oil	¼ cup	steak sauce
1	red onion, diced	2 tbsp.	lemon juice
4 cloves	garlic, chopped		Salt and pepper to taste
2 tbsp.	chopped fresh thyme	6	sea bass fillets (each 6 oz.)
2	green onions, finely chopped	1 tbsp.	Bay Seasoning (page 98)
½ cup	gourmet BBQ sauce		

1. In a medium saucepan heat the olive oil over medium-high heat. Sauté the onion and garlic for 2 to 3 minutes or until tender. Add the thyme and green onions; cook, stirring, for 1 minute. Add BBQ sauce, steak sauce and lemon juice. Bring to a boil, reduce heat to medium-low and simmer for 15 minutes, stirring occasionally. Season with salt and pepper. Pour into a glass dish large enough to hold the fish and let cool.

2. Season fillets with Bay Seasoning, pressing the seasoning into the flesh. Add to the marinade, turning to coat. Cover and let marinate at room temperature for 1 hour.

3. Preheat grill to medium-high.

4. Remove fillets from marinade, reserving marinade. Grill for 5 to 6 minutes per side, basting liberally with the marinade.

SERVES 6

Grilled Halibut T-Bone Steaks with Grapefruit Avocado Butter Sauce

The T-bone steak of the sea is just as flavourful as a steak.

1 cup	grapefruit juice	2	green onions, finely chopped
¼ cup	olive oil	1	jalapeño pepper, finely chopped
2 tbsp.	chopped fresh tarragon		Sea salt to taste
1 tbsp.	cracked black pepper	6	halibut T-bone steaks (each 8 oz.)
1 tsp.	mustard powder	½	grapefruit
2	shallots, finely chopped		

1. In a glass dish large enough to hold the fish, whisk together the grapefruit juice, olive oil, tarragon, black pepper, mustard powder, shallots, green onions, jalapeño and salt. Add halibut, turning to coat. Cover and marinate at room temperature for 1 hour.

2. Preheat grill to medium-high.

3. Remove halibut from marinade, reserving marinade for basting. Grill for 5 to 6 minutes per side or until the centre bone of the halibut can be pulled cleanly from the meat, basting frequently with the marinade.

4. When the halibut is cooked, squeeze the grapefruit juice over the fish.

5. Serve with Grapefruit Avocado Butter Sauce (recipe follows).

SERVES 6

Grapefruit Avocado Butter Sauce

6 tbsp.	cold butter (4 tbsp. cut in pieces)	1	grapefruit, peeled and segmented
4	shallots, chopped	1	avocado, diced
2 cloves	garlic, chopped	1 tbsp.	chopped fresh parsley
½ cup	grapefruit juice		Salt and pepper
¼ cup	Riesling white wine		

1. In a small saucepan over medium-high heat, melt 2 tbsp. of the butter. Sauté the shallots and garlic for 2 minutes or until tender. Add the grapefruit juice and wine. Bring to a boil and reduce the liquid by half.

2. Reduce heat to low and whisk in the remaining butter until smooth.

3. Gently stir in the grapefruit, avocado and parsley. Season to taste with salt and pepper.

MAKES ABOUT 1 CUP

Tuna Pepper Steak

Tuna steaks are one of the easiest seafoods to grill. Their firm texture allows for easy preparation. The less you cook firm-fleshed fish like tuna, swordfish and marlin, the tastier it will be.

6	tuna steaks (each 1½ inches thick and 6 oz.)	½ cup	oyster sauce
		¼ cup	rice wine vinegar
¼ cup	Malabar Pepper Rub (page 96)	¼ cup	honey
¼ cup	olive oil	2	green onions, finely chopped

1. Preheat grill to high.

2. Rub the tuna steaks with the Malabar pepper seasoning, pressing the seasoning into the fish. Brush steaks with olive oil.

3. In a bowl stir together the oyster sauce, vinegar, honey and green onions.

4. Grill the tuna steaks for 2 minutes per side for rare, basting with the oyster sauce glaze.

5. Slice the tuna steaks and serve with Sesame Shrimp and Snap Pea Salad (page 31), if desired.

SERVES 6

Sugarcane-Skewered Swordfish with Lemon Honey Glaze

The natural sweetness of sugarcane blends well with the firm texture of swordfish. This is an easy recipe that can be prepared in minutes. Look for sugarcane in grocery stores or specialty markets.

1	stick fresh sugarcane (8 inches long), peeled and quartered	¼ cup	olive oil
		¼ cup	lemon juice
4	centre-cut swordfish steaks (each 1½ inches thick and 8 oz.)	¼ cup	honey
		1 tbsp.	chopped fresh cilantro
1 tbsp.	Bay Seasoning (page 98)		Salt and pepper to taste

1. Preheat grill to medium-high.

2. Using a sharp knife, cut a point on one end of each sugarcane skewer. Insert 1 sugarcane skewer into the side of each swordfish steak.

3. Season the swordfish with Bay Seasoning and then brush with olive oil. Set aside.

4. In a small bowl whisk together the lemon juice, honey, cilantro, salt and pepper.

5. Grill swordfish for 3 to 4 minutes per side for medium-rare, brushing liberally with the lemon honey glaze.

SERVES 4

Cinnamon-Skewered Scallops with Brown Sugar Butter and Peach-Orange Salsa

The idea for this recipe came from my chef friend Niall Hill. Niall is working his culinary charms in Ireland and has a flare for great-tasting food. I call him the sexy chef, for his food is full of passion. Marrying scallops and cinnamon sticks may seem odd, but the two go perfectly well together. Soaking the cinnamon sticks not only prevents burning but extracts more cinnamon flavour.

BROWN SUGAR BUTTER

½ cup	butter, softened
3 tbsp.	sultana raisins
2 tbsp.	brown sugar
2 tbsp.	orange juice
½ tsp.	chopped fresh thyme

PEACH-ORANGE SALSA

2	oranges
4	peaches, peeled and thinly sliced
1	red bell pepper, diced
1	jalapeño pepper, seeded and finely chopped
1	shallot, finely chopped

¼ cup	orange blossom honey
2 tbsp.	Grand Marnier
2 tbsp.	olive oil
2 tsp.	chopped fresh cilantro
	Salt and freshly ground black pepper to taste

6	cinnamon sticks (each at least 5 inches long)
24	jumbo sea scallops
⅓ cup	orange juice
⅓ cup	olive oil
2 tbsp.	Indonesian Cinnamon Rub (page 108)
1 tbsp.	rice vinegar
	Salt to taste

1. Soak the cinnamon sticks for at least 1 hour.

2. To prepare the brown sugar butter, in a small bowl combine the butter, raisins, brown sugar, orange juice and thyme. Mix until well blended. Cover and refrigerate.

3. To prepare the peach-orange salsa, grate 1 tsp. zest from an orange. Set aside. Peel and segment oranges, removing membranes. In a large bowl combine the orange zest and segments, peaches, red pepper, jalapeño, shallot, honey, Grand Marnier, olive oil, cilantro, salt and black pepper. Cover and refrigerate.

Continued ...

Tip

Try skewering lamb, chicken, beef or turkey with cinnamon sticks for a boost of flavour.

4. Skewer 4 scallops onto each cinnamon stick. Place in one layer in a glass dish.

5. In a small bowl stir together the orange juice, olive oil, Indonesian Cinnamon Rub, rice vinegar and salt.
Pour over the scallop skewers, turning to coat. Marinate, covered and refrigerated, for 30 minutes.

6. Preheat grill to medium-high. (If you wish, use a grill screen to prevent the skewers from falling through the grill.)

7. Remove scallops from marinade, reserving marinade, and grill for 2 to 4 minutes per side or until scallops are just cooked through, basting with the marinade.

8. Serve each skewer with a tablespoon of the brown sugar butter and one-sixth of the peach-orange salsa.

SERVES 6

Grilled Crab-Stuffed Jumbo Shrimp with Papaya Sauce

For this recipe you will need extra-large jumbo shrimp, which are a lot easier to stuff than small shrimp.

1 cup	fresh crab meat, drained		2	green onions, finely chopped
⅓ cup	firm ricotta cheese		2 cloves	garlic, chopped
2 tbsp.	lemon juice			Salt and pepper to taste
1 tbsp.	chopped fresh cilantro		8	extra-large jumbo shrimp (3–5 per lb.),
2 tsp.	Bay Seasoning (page 98)			tail on, peeled and deveined
1	egg, lightly beaten		1½ cups	cornflake crumbs
3	shallots, finely diced			

1. In a large bowl mix together thoroughly the crab meat, ricotta cheese, lemon juice, cilantro, Bay Seasoning, egg, shallots, green onions, garlic, salt and pepper. Cover and refrigerate.

2. Preheat grill to high.

3. Using a sharp knife, cut along the back of each shrimp almost all the way through to butterfly the shrimp. Gently spread the meat apart to make a cavity. Season the shrimp with salt and pepper.

4. Fill each shrimp with 2 to 3 tbsp. of the crab stuffing, pressing firmly. Sprinkle the stuffed shrimp with cornflake crumbs and press gently so they adhere.

5. Grill shrimp for 3 to 5 minutes. Carefully move shrimp to the cool side of the grill for indirect cooking and cook the shrimp for 4 to 5 more minutes or until they are firm but not tough and the stuffing is hot.

6. Serve with Papaya Sauce (recipe follows).

SERVES 4

Papaya Sauce

1	ripe papaya, peeled and seeded	1 tbsp.	sugar
1	large orange, juiced	1 tsp.	hot sauce (optional)
½ cup	grapeseed oil		Salt and pepper to taste

1. In a food processor or blender, purée the papaya and orange juice until very smooth.

2. While still puréeing, slowly add the oil until fully incorporated.

3. Add sugar, hot sauce, salt and pepper. Pulse to blend.

4. Transfer to a bowl, cover and refrigerate until needed.

MAKES ABOUT 2 CUPS

Hot and Spicy Grilled Shrimp

The shrimp-loving heat-seekers among you will go for this recipe big time! To increase the heat even more, add a finely chopped jalapeño or Scotch bonnet pepper.

2 lb.	jumbo shrimp (12–15 per lb.), peeled and deveined	2 tbsp.	Worcestershire Sauce
		4	green onions, finely chopped
2 tbsp.	Bay Seasoning (page 98)	4 cloves	garlic, finely chopped
1 cup	ketchup	1	lemon, juiced
2 tbsp.	brown sugar		Salt and pepper to taste
2 tbsp.	chopped fresh cilantro		Lime wedges, for garnish
2 tbsp.	hot sauce		

1. Soak six 8- to 10-inch bamboo skewers in warm water for 1 hour. (Or use metal skewers.)

2. In a large bowl toss the shrimp with the Bay Seasoning, making sure to coat all of the shrimp.

3. Thread 5 or 6 shrimp onto each skewer and place in a glass dish large enough to hold the skewers in one layer.

4. In a bowl stir together the ketchup, brown sugar, cilantro, hot sauce, Worcestershire sauce, green onions, garlic, lemon juice, salt and pepper. Pour half of this mixture over the shrimp and marinate for at least 15 minutes. Reserve the remaining sauce for basting.

5. Preheat grill to medium-high.

6. On a well-seasoned grill, grill the shrimp for 2 to 3 minutes per side or until opaque and just cooked through, basting with reserved marinade.

7. Serve immediately with lime wedges.

SERVES 6

Grilled Oysters with Mango BBQ Sauce

I prepared this recipe for the Taste of CART Chef Competition at the Mid Ohio Race in August 2000. This was one of the recipes that helped me win the competition.

18	fresh oysters	1 tbsp.	chopped fresh ginger
1	mango, peeled, seeded and diced	1 tbsp.	lime juice
3 cloves	garlic, minced	Dash	hot sauce
1 cup	gourmet BBQ sauce		Salt and pepper
2 tbsp.	chopped fresh cilantro	9 slices	bacon
2 tbsp.	vegetable oil	2 cups	shredded Monterey Jack cheese

1. To shuck the oysters, grip each oyster flat side up in a folded kitchen towel. Find a small opening between the shells near the hinge and pry open with an oyster knife. Carefully remove the top shell and discard or use for decoration. Holding the oyster over a bowl to catch the liquor, loosen the oyster from the shell by running the oyster knife underneath the body. Carefully remove the oyster from the shell and drain on paper towels. Set aside the shell bottoms.

2. In a medium saucepan combine the oyster liquor, mango, garlic, BBQ sauce, cilantro, oil, ginger, lime juice and hot sauce. Bring to a boil, reduce heat and simmer, stirring occasionally, for 10 minutes. In a blender or food processor, purée until smooth. Season to taste with salt and pepper. Set sauce aside.

3. Preheat grill to medium-high.

4. Fry the bacon until it is just cooked but not crisp. Drain on paper towels and cut each slice in half.

5. Wrap each oyster with a half-slice of bacon and place in a reserved oyster shell. Top each oyster with a tablespoon of mango BBQ sauce and sprinkle each with Monterey Jack cheese.

6. Place the oyster shells on the grill and close the lid. Grill for 10 minutes.

SERVES 6

Grilled Garlic Beer Butter Lobster Tails

For this recipe I like to use big, meaty Caribbean lobster tails. On a recent trip to Antigua I prepared this recipe on the beach one evening for my love, Pamela, and me. Succulent lobster tails basted with garlic butter and beer … couldn't ask for much more.

4	frozen Caribbean lobster tails (each 8 oz.)	2 tbsp.	lemon juice
4 tsp.	Bay Seasoning (page 98)	1 tbsp.	chopped fresh dill
1 cup	beer	8 cloves	garlic, minced
½ cup	butter		Salt and pepper to taste

1. Partially thaw the lobster tails. Using a sharp knife, cut down the centre of each tail—into the meat but not all the way through. Spread the tail open to butterfly it. Season each tail with the Bay Seasoning.

2. Place a sheet of foil on the grill and heat to medium-high.

3. In a small saucepan combine the beer, butter, lemon juice, dill and garlic. Slowly heat, stirring, until the butter is melted and the sauce is hot.

4. Brush the lobster tails with the garlic beer butter sauce and place meat side down on the foil. Grill for 6 to 7 minutes, basting with sauce, until the meat is opaque and just cooked. Do not overcook the tails or they will be tough.

5. Serve the lobster with the remaining sauce for dipping.

SERVES 2 TO 4 WITH LOTS OF CHAMPAGNE

Decadent Delights

Desserts

Drinks

Grilled Pineapple with Molasses Rum Glaze

Grilling pineapple brings out its natural sugars. Grilled pineapple makes a great dessert but it's also wonderful when used in BBQ sauces and salsas.

1	ripe pineapple	1 tsp.	cracked black pepper
½ cup	molasses	½ tsp.	ground mace
¼ cup	dark rum		Coconut ice cream
¼ cup	orange juice		

---

1. Using a sharp knife, cut top and bottom off the pineapple. Stand pineapple upright and, slicing from top to bottom, remove the skin. Cut out any sharp "eyes." Cut pineapple in half lengthwise. Set aside.

2. Preheat grill to medium-high.

3. In a small saucepan bring the molasses, rum, orange juice, pepper and mace to a boil. Reduce heat and simmer, stirring, for 5 minutes.

4. Grill the pineapple cut side down for 10 minutes, basting with the molasses mixture. Reduce heat to medium-low, close the lid and grill for another 10 to 15 minutes or until golden brown, hot and tender.

5. Use tongs and a spatula to carefully transfer the pineapple to a cutting board. Slice each half crosswise into 12 slices. Serve 3 or 4 slices of pineapple with coconut ice cream.

SERVES 8

Lydia's BBQ Baked Banana Boats

My friend Lydia made this ooey gooey delight for me at the cottage one summer. This is her favourite summertime recipe. Thanks, Lydia, for all the summer days at Wasaga Beach.

4	bananas, unpeeled	¼ cup	chopped pecans
¼ cup	semisweet chocolate chips	1 cup	mini marshmallows
¼ cup	butterscotch chips		Vanilla ice cream

1. Preheat grill to high.

2. Using a sharp knife, make 2 incisions about 1 inch apart along the inside curve of the banana and remove and discard the strip of peel. Gently pull open the remaining peel but do not remove it.

3. Cut the banana (not the peel) into 1-inch-thick rounds, leaving the fruit in the peel.

4. Mix together the chocolate chips, butterscotch chips and pecans. Push the mixture between the banana slices. Top with mini marshmallows. Wrap each stuffed banana in heavy-duty foil.

5. Place the banana boats on the grill and close the lid. Bake for 8 minutes or until the bananas are tender and the chocolate and butterscotch chips and the marshmallows have melted.

6. Carefully open the foil. Serve with vanilla ice cream.

SERVES 4

Grilled Lemon Pound Cake with Stewed Summer Berry Pot

Create some great grilled flavours with this lemony pound cake. Lightly grilled pound cake is the perfect match for stewed summer berries.

3 cups	all-purpose flour	6	medium eggs
½ tsp.	baking powder	1 cup	milk
1 cup +		2 tbsp.	lemon juice
3 tbsp.	butter, softened	1½ tsp.	vanilla
½ cup	shortening	1 tsp.	lemon zest
3 cups	sugar		

1. Preheat oven to 325°F. Grease and flour an 8- or 10-inch tube pan.

2. Sift together the flour and baking powder.

3. In a mixing bowl, cream the butter, shortening and sugar until smooth. Add the eggs and beat well.

4. Add the flour, alternating with the milk. Stir in the vanilla, lemon zest, and lemon juice.

5. Turn batter into tube pan. Bake for 1½ hours or until a tester comes out clean. Let cool on a rack.

6. Preheat grill to medium.

7. Run a knife around the edge of the pan, invert and remove pound cake. Slice the cake into 1- to 2-inch-thick slices. Lightly butter both sides.

8. Grill for 1 to 2 minutes per side or until lightly golden and toasted.

9. Serve with Stewed Summer Berry Pot (recipe follows) and a spoonful of vanilla or coconut ice cream.

SERVES 8

Stewed Summer Berry Pot

My friend Olaf finds that this is a great way to use up leftover summer berries. Waste not, want not!
This is also terrific on ice cream.

1 pint	raspberries	2 cups	cranberry juice
½ pint	red currants	½ cup	sugar
½ pint	blueberries	1	cinnamon stick
1½ cups	pitted sour cherries	1	orange, juice and zest
1½ cups	sliced strawberries	1½ tbsp.	quick-cooking tapioca
2 cups	dry red wine		

1. In a mixing bowl, gently toss together the raspberries, red currants, blueberries, sour cherries and strawberries. Transfer 2 cups of the berries to a food processor and purée.

2. In a large saucepan mix the berry purée with the red wine, cranberry juice, sugar, cinnamon stick, orange juice and orange zest. Bring to a boil, stirring. Reduce heat and simmer, stirring occasionally, for 15 minutes. Stir in the tapioca and return to a boil, stirring until thick.

3. Strain the berry mixture through a fine sieve set over a bowl, reserving the liquid. Pour the hot liquid over the fresh berries and gently fold together.

MAKES 8 CUPS

Grilled Peaches with Bourbon Honey

Fresh sweet peaches are meant for the grill. Lightly warmed and charred, then drizzled with bourbon-infused honey, they're a real summer treat.

6	ripe peaches	¼ cup	honey
2 tbsp.	grapeseed oil	¼ cup	bourbon
¼ tsp.	nutmeg		Vanilla ice cream
	Cracked black pepper to taste		

1. Preheat grill to medium-high.

2. Slice the peaches in half and remove the pit. Brush the peach halves with grapeseed oil. Season with nutmeg and black pepper. Set aside.

3. In a small saucepan over low heat, warm the honey and bourbon, stirring until blended.

4. Grill the peach halves cut side down for 3 to 4 minutes or until lightly charred and warm. Turn, baste with bourbon honey mixture and grill for 5 more minutes or until fully cooked and tender.

5. Serve peach halves with a scoop of vanilla ice cream and drizzled with remaining bourbon honey.

SERVES 6

Rhubarb and Bourbon Fool

This recipe appeared in the *Ottawa Citizen* a few years ago after Food Editor Ron Eade asked me to create a few fool recipes. This light and easy recipe blends tart rhubarb with delicious bourbon.

1 lb.	fresh rhubarb, cut in 1-inch pieces	Pinch	cinnamon
¼ cup	water	2 cups	whipping cream
½ cup	(approx.) sugar	½ cup	chocolate chips
¼ cup	bourbon		Cracked black pepper to taste

1. In a medium saucepan over medium-high heat simmer the rhubarb and water, covered and stirring occasionally, for 10 to 15 minutes or until the rhubarb is tender.

2. Stir in the sugar to taste. Simmer for 10 more minutes.

3. Remove from heat and stir in the bourbon and cinnamon. Let cool completely, then chill.

4. When the rhubarb is cold, in a large bowl whip the cream to stiff peaks. Gently fold the rhubarb and chocolate chips into the whipped cream, being careful not to overmix.

5. Spoon fool into 6 chilled serving glasses and garnish with black pepper.

SERVES 6

Dark Chocolate Orange Bread Pudding with Whisky Orange Compote

I first prepared this dessert for the U.S. ambassador to Canada with then Ambassador Chef Corey Haskins. The richness of buttery croissants and chocolate is truly decadent!

16	day-old croissants (or 1 baguette), cut into 1-inch pieces		½ cup	coarsely chopped pecans
			2 tbsp.	brown sugar
2 cups	milk			
2 cups	orange juice		**WHISKY ORANGE COMPOTE**	
2 cups	granulated sugar		3 cups	orange juice
2 tbsp.	vanilla		½ cup	sugar
1 tsp.	cinnamon		½ cup	Canadian whisky
1 tsp.	nutmeg		2 tsp.	cornstarch
3	eggs		2 tbsp.	cold water
1½ cups	coarsely chopped bitter or semisweet chocolate		2	oranges, peeled and segmented

1. Preheat oven to 350°F. Grease a 13- x 9- x 2-inch baking pan.

2. Place croissant pieces in a large bowl. Pour milk and orange juice over croissants. Let stand 20 minutes or until liquid is absorbed. Spread croissant pieces evenly in baking dish.

3. In a medium bowl whisk sugar, vanilla, cinnamon, nutmeg and eggs together until thick. Stir in chocolate and pecans.

4. Pour over croissant pieces. Sprinkle with brown sugar.

5. Bake for 50 to 60 minutes or until just set and a knife comes out clean. Let pudding stand for 10 minutes before serving.

6. While bread pudding is baking, make orange compote. In a medium saucepan over medium-high heat, bring the orange juice, sugar and whisky to a boil, stirring. Reduce heat to medium and simmer for 5 minutes.

7. Stir the cornstarch into 2 tablespoons of cold water until smooth. Stir into juice mixture and simmer, stirring, for 5 minutes or until thick. Stir in orange segments; simmer for 5 more minutes.

8. Serve compote warm with the chocolate orange bread pudding.

SERVES 8 TO 10

Cast-Iron-Baked Strawberry Apple Crisp

Using your grill as an oven keeps you from heating up your kitchen on those warm summer days.

4 cups	sliced strawberries	¾ cup	brown sugar
3 cups	peeled, cored and thinly sliced apples	½ cup	all-purpose flour
		½ tsp.	cinnamon
½ cup	sugar	½ tsp.	ground mace
¼ cup	amaretto	½ cup	butter
¾ cup	rolled oats	½ cup	chopped pecans

1. Preheat grill to medium. Butter an 8- to 10-inch cast-iron frying pan.

2. In a large bowl toss together the strawberries, apples, sugar and amaretto. Pour the fruit mixture into the cast-iron pan.

3. Wipe out the bowl and in it combine the oats, brown sugar, flour, cinnamon and mace. Cut in the butter until mixture resembles coarse crumbs. Stir in the pecans. Sprinkle the topping over the fruit.

4. Place crumble on the grill and close the lid. Bake for 50 to 60 minutes or until the fruit is soft and the topping is crisp and golden brown. Let stand for 15 minutes.

5. Serve with ice cream.

SERVES 8

Island Pink Lemonade Rum Punch

While in Jamaica I had this refreshing rum punch at a beach bar. It's a great way to wash down some spicy jerk pork.

1	can (12 oz.) frozen concentrated pink lemonade
24 oz.	water
1	can ginger ale
1 cup	dark rum
8 sprigs	mint
2	lemons, thinly sliced
1 pint	raspberries

1. In a large pitcher place the concentrated pink lemonade. Add 2 lemonade cans of water, ginger ale, rum, mint and lemon slices. Stir to blend.

2. Add the raspberries and fill with ice.

3. Serve immediately.

SERVES 8

Tequila Honey Orange Cooler

I first made this delicious drink with a wonderful product called Honeydew, a frozen concentrated orange drink with honey. It's a real summertime treat. If you can find Honeydew, use it in place of the orange juice. Don't leave out the honey, though. This drink still needs it.

1 cup	crushed ice
1 cup	orange juice
¼ cup	gold tequila
2 tbsp.	honey
2	maraschino cherries
1 tsp.	cherry syrup
2 sprigs	mint
2 tbsp.	Grand Marnier

1. Place the crushed ice in a cocktail shaker. Add the orange juice, tequila and honey. Shake it up big time, baby.

2. Place 1 cherry, ½ tsp. of cherry syrup and 1 sprig of mint in each of 2 martini glasses.

3. Strain tequila mix into glasses. Top each with 1 tbsp. of Grand Marnier and serve.

SERVES 2

Sour Cherry Bourbon Coolers

When fresh sour cherries are in season, make this cooler. It is best if you let the cherries soak in the bourbon for two or three days to allow for the fullest flavour.

24	pitted sour cherries
1½ cups	bourbon
2 cups	black cherry juice
2	cans cola
8 sprigs	fresh mint

1. Place the sour cherries in a large jar. Pour the bourbon over the cherries. Seal the jar and refrigerate for 2 or 3 days.

2. Fill 8 large glasses with ice. Place 3 of the soaked cherries in each glass. Equally divide the bourbon among the glasses.

3. Pour ¼ cup of the black cherry juice into each glass.

4. Top with cola and garnish with fresh mint.

SERVES 8

Maple Carrot Iced Tea

Carrots have a natural sweetness that is ideal for this summertime drink. You can also replace the carrots with fresh peeled beets. The results are delicious — and the colour is outstanding.

4 cups	water
½ cup	maple syrup
6	large carrots, peeled and shredded
1	green apple, peeled and sliced
2	oranges, juiced
1	lemon, juiced
6	black peppercorns
4 sprigs	thyme

1. In a large saucepan bring the water and maple syrup to a boil. Add the carrots, apple, orange juice, lemon juice and peppercorns. Return to a boil. Remove from the heat and let steep for 30 minutes.

2. Strain, discarding the solids, and chill.

3. Serve over ice with a sprig of fresh thyme.

SERVES 4

Index